HAVING MY CAKE

THE MASTERY OF MINDFUL EATING

ISBN-13: 978-0692235768

ISBN -10: 0692235760

Cover photo and photo of author both courtesy of Daniel Reichert Photography. www.DanielReichert.com

Having my Cake

The Mastery of Mindful Eating

by Karen Wexler

This book is dedicated to my sister, Judy, who taught me the practice of moderation decades ago. Every Halloween, she would take her loot and decide which piece of candy she would have each night, allowing herself one a day, so that her stash would last for months. I would finish off my entire bag within a week and was always so jealous to see she still had candy well into the new year, while all I had was a stomach ache from eating too much at once.

Special thanks to: Daniel Reichert, David Jay Smith Chang, Greg Kachejian, Judith Kelman, Sherry Suib Cohen, Joseph DeFilippis, Melissa Kalt, Catherine Canade, Tracy Kane, Michael Kowalski and Michael Mercier.

CONTENTS

Introduction

At a recent annual physical, my internist, an early forty-something woman, looked at me with admiration and said, "I see you are as slender as ever. How do you stay thin? What is your secret?" This was coming from a physician. I took a breath and looked her squarely in the face and replied, "M&Ms. Nothing but M&Ms before 5 pm." Then I got serious and explained that I don't eat more food than I need to, I try to eat mostly nutritious, high quality food, and I exercise regularly. That's my secret. There it is, America. There's no secret at all. That kind of sucks, right? No! It's actually good news. Managing your weight is about creating a healthy balance and it IS within your power.

Your body tells you when it doesn't need more food. You used to pay attention to the signs, when you were an infant. When you needed food, your body signaled you and you cried. You didn't think about that last piece of apple pie in the fridge and then go and do some damage. You couldn't walk, and thankfully so!

This book is about common sense. No diets, no fads, no magic secrets. It's science and art. How many calories does it take to sustain someone with your height and weight and activity level? I only require about 1400-1600 calories. If I eat more than I need and don't burn it off, I will gain weight. I work at it. I watch *what* I eat. Am I obsessed? No, but usually I think about what I put in my body. Do I always eat healthy foods? No. But I eat most foods in moderation, especially when I know certain foods will make me fat if I eat too much of them. Do I deprive myself of any one food? Not on your life. Eating is too enjoyable. I am a pretty smart eater, and I am happy to share my strategies if you'd like to come along for the ride.

I want my readers to incorporate the foods they love to eat into a healthy, sensible way of eating. This book is not meant to disregard or make light of anyone's personal struggle with food. I also appreciate that in modern society, with all of the ready-made foods at our disposal, it is an extremely difficult atmosphere in which to make wise eating choices. I believe in abolishing the concepts of "good" and "bad" foods as I fear that only serves to make certain foods seem forbidden and thus, more enticing. My hope is that reading how I eat, how I plan what I am going to eat and how I daily make conscious decisions about what I put in my body, will encourage others to do the same and create more of an informed eating culture among us.

First, I don't want to frustrate you or have you think that learning to eat mindfully is too big a hill to climb. You can only get to the top of Everest by taking one step at a time, right? So start walking. At least give this a shot because chances are, if you're reading this book, you have not been satisfied with your prior attempts to keep your weight down or to have a healthier relationship with food. I'm forty-eight years old and I don't loathe my body. I think it looks pretty good most of the time. I had a period in the 80s when I struggled with maintaining my weight. I had the dreaded "freshman fifteen", but give me a break-they had at least fifteen different kinds of cereal in college and I would mix them in one big bowl. After those college years, I found a successful balance that combined what I needed to eat with what I wanted to eat. Downing a row of *Oreos* is not something you will catch me doing these days, however, I do have my poisons. Like you, there are foods that, if I could eat them all day long and not gain a pound, I would. Heath bars, Junior Mints and cheese would be up there. Perhaps there is something you can learn from me. I'm not perfect, but I am really good at this thing of maintaining my weight. I think I can help you.

I'm 5 feet tall and I have a slight build. Don't hate me. Just because I'm small doesn't mean I have it easy. Think about it, I need to eat less than most people because my body doesn't require as much food to sustain itself as a larger person's does. Therefore, I have to be even more vigilant about watching what I put into my mouth. So who better to learn from than me? You may be naturally fleshy and curvy or thick and stocky and not have the frame of a thin person. Everyone doesn't have to be thin, that is not the goal of this book, nor is it realistic. I'm talking about being at a healthy weight for your body type. That's all. You'll feel better, look better and chances are you will be healthier overall.

CHAPTER ONE

The Unmindful Day

Every morning when we wake up, we have the opportunity to start fresh. We can make good decisions or we can make lousy ones. Either way, all is not lost, as come tomorrow we get the same chance to start over. If you make poor decisions day after day after day, then the consequences may appear on your body as a muffin top, love handles, thunder thighs and other phrases that we despise. Below is an example of how I might have a particularly bad day of eating:

1. 7:05 am. My apartment. I'm up and at 'em. I have been sleeping for almost seven hours, I hope, and wake up *famished*. I turn the water on for my shower and don't think I can wait until I am showered to have breakfast. I look in the fridge and see a leftover half of whoopee pie and I scarf it down on the way to the shower, no doubt leaving a trail of crumbs in my haste. Boy, that's good. I like to start the day sweetly. That whoopee pie has 35 grams of sugar[1] so I'm starting out with half of that, about 17 grams. There are approximately four grams of sugar in each teaspoon. The Mayo Clinic indicates that in order to keep levels of triglycerides, or fat in the blood, at safe levels, women should have no more than 6 teaspoons of added sugar per day, men, no more than 9.[2] That means I've already had 4 of my 6 teaspoons of added sugar and I'm not even dressed. Nice job.

---

[1] Based on nutritional information listed for Trader Joe's Chocolate Whoopee Pies.

[2] From the Mayo Clinic's website topic "Added Sugars: Don't get Sabotaged by Sweeteners".

2. 7:25 am. Out of shower and ready to eat breakfast. Time for cereal.

I keep only healthy, low sugar cereals in the house and sometimes sprinkle a little something fun on it, say a few dark chocolate chips. This morning, however, I see I have a leftover bag of peanut M&Ms hanging around and I make the stellar decision to pour the remaining half bag onto my multigrain oatbran flakes. My sugar intake just went over my day's limit.

3. 9:02 am. I'm at a work meeting where breakfast is being served and I

cannot resist the frosted Danish pastry. They do have some assorted fruit options and some bagels and cream cheese but I like the sweet stuff and I'm in that kind of mood. Let's say I've got pms too; that's likely what's kicking my sugar craving into high gear. I didn't have a chance to grab my tea this morning so I help myself to a cup of decaf coffee and put cream and two sugars in it. I'll be riding my sugar high until about ten or eleven and then I'll drop .

4. 10:45 am. I'm in the office at my desk and feeling sluggish and hungry. I forgot to bring a plain Greek yogurt so I'm checking in with my coworkers to see who's got what today. I work with some good cooks and bakers (myself included, thank you very much) and often there's something homemade around. Today, there's baklava and crusty bread from the French bakery down the block. And jam. In an effort to make it until lunch, I have a two-inch piece of the very sweet baklava and then a one inch thick slice of the crusty bread. I forego the jam. I've eaten more carbs and sugars and have done very little to satisfy my hunger. I'm a mess today.

5. 12:15 pm. Time for lunch. I know you're wondering if I ever get work done, but I do. It is perfectly understandable that I would be

starving at noon when I've consumed mostly sugars all morning with not so much protein or fiber, save the peanuts in the M&Ms and the cereal. I make my way to the cafeteria (and I take the steps, not the escalator, at least there's that to salvage my pride) and see they have spaghetti and meatballs, grilled chicken breast with bruschetta topping and some gross white fish with weird spices. I go for the spaghetti, of course. It's just that kind of day. I notice they are serving spinach so I also take some cooked spinach but I avoid the salad bar, thinking that will be too much.

When I return to my desk and begin eating, I eat one and a half of the three meatballs and only half of the spinach. I feel kind of gross. I'm full, but not satisfied or nourished. I do finish the pasta though; it is so easy to eat. At least I'm drinking only water and not a sugary soda or sweetened ice tea. I am about to reach into my bottom desk drawer to grab a couple of cookies when my colleague pokes her head in my office to announce that Chris down the hall has made his delicious lemon squares. They're small; I think to myself, one won't kill me.

6. 2:45pm. I'm upstairs in the hospital on one of the inpatient floors and
am grabbed by the arm and pulled into a conference room to sing "Happy Birthday" to one of the nurses. I do my best to sing the harmony full and strong. I am successful. I am offered cake. Seven layer chocolate cake with buttercream frosting. Yes. I take a small slice as I am beginning to feel that the waistband on my pantyhose is sawing me in half.   Mindless, mindless eating...

7. 4:35 pm. I'm at my desk again and feeling that I need a little something before I go home. I remember I have a bag of jellybeans in my desk drawer and I take a small handful with a little

piece of dark chocolate, one of my favorite combos.

8. 6:20 pm. I am doing some errands in my neighborhood after work and realize that I forgot to go grocery shopping this past weekend. I have no plan for dinner. I stop at Tony's for what I think is going to be a chicken cutlet and some salad perhaps but the many pizzas offered catch my eye. I settle on two Grandma slices, which are crispy, flat, square-shaped margherita pizzas- red sauce and cheese, no meat or veggies. I figure I can put together a salad when I get home. When I arrive home, I see only celery and some wilted romaine in the crisper but I chop it up and put a little olive oil and balsamic vinegar on it.

9.   7:45pm. My kitchen. Wanting a little something sweet to end my meal. I have some nerve, I know. But have pity on mindless Me because I haven't been paying attention to my

choices today. No one thing seemed that awful and the portions seemed reasonable. I will have one small homemade chocolate chip cookie and then call it a night. Ok, two cookies.

Tomorrow is another day.

Who knows how much sugar I consumed today? I was an animal. I ate what was in front of me and what was convenient, with very little thought. I probably ate more sugar today than I should have in a week. I had very little protein and lots of empty calories. I did get a couple of veggies in and at least I started out with some fiber and whole grains. All is not lost. I'm not proud of this day, but the good news is that tomorrow brings with it the possibility of a more mindful me.

CHAPTER TWO

Who the Hell Am I to Tell You How to Eat?

You are probably wondering what my qualifications are to be telling you how to eat. Why did this woman decide her thoughts were worth putting into print to be read by lots and lots of people? I have a masters degree in health advocacy and have worked the past fifteen years as a patient advocate in a hospital setting. My work tends to focus on assisting patients and their families after a person has already been diagnosed with an illness. I would like now to be involved in a more proactive way, by helping people take control of their health to try to prevent illness. Obesity, for example, is a condition that increases a person's chance of complications during treatment for life-threatening illnesses. We are also aware that childhood obesity is at an all-time high and that we as a nation are fatter than we have ever been, despite a cultural shift decades ago to a low-fat diet. How are we going to change this trend?

Oh, hold it one second. One thing first: my promise to you, dear reader, is that each time I take a break for a snack or a meal while I'm writing this book, I am going to honestly tell you what I'm eating, when I'm eating and how much I'm eating. I think this will help you to understand how I maintain my weight.

I am a bit hungry and have not had dinner, so I am going to make a peanut butter and jelly sandwich on some whole grain flax seed bread with some celery sticks on the side. I am putting on about 1 tablespoon of organic crunchy peanut butter - nothing but peanuts and salt - and the same of Polaner All-fruit

Strawberry preserves with two stalks of celery and one 8 oz. glass of water.

I have been playing with fonts and formatting the past several minutes, and now I want a little something sweet and rich, so I'm taking a four ounce dish and filling it 2/3 full with fresh strawberries and blueberries. Next, I'm adding two rounded tablespoons of Hagen Dazs chocolate chocolate chip ice cream. Note I said TABLESPOONS, not ice cream *scoopfuls*. That's not much folks. Just a little taste of the richness is all I have come to need. I feel like I am having a yummy dessert and, in fact, I am enjoying the creamy deliciousness of the ice cream I love so much without overdoing it. I do not feel deprived; I feel indulgent, but in a smart, fairly healthful way, since I'm adding the berries with their fiber and vitamins and antioxidants. I know I probably will not eat much of anything else for the rest of the evening. Because I ate very slowly, I savored every bite and likely I will not feel hungry later. If I do get hungry, I will allow myself a handful of Kashi Cinnamon Harvest bites whole-wheat cereal, a few almonds, walnuts or a raw vegetable. That is it; I am eating nothing again until morning. No late night snacking on chips or cookies or candy or half of a ham sandwich. The only "candy" I generally keep in the house is dark chocolate. I always find it is best not to be tempted. Who wouldn't throw back a few handfuls of M&Ms if they were around? (Remember Chapter One?)

Ok, I seriously digressed. I believe we can alter the very disturbing path we are on by changing the mindset of each individual. We need to regain respect for our bodies and our lives and learn to live, once again, by a simple philosophy which served our ancestors well before we had all of the ready-to-eat foods that we now have available: eat only what your body needs.

I certainly do not mean to take the fun out of eating. I will show you how to enjoy all of the foods that you love, but in portions that do not put your body over the edge. I have often wondered why people seem obsessed with how much they can eat. Perhaps I have never had this fascination with non-stop eating because I grew up in a family where we usually ate our meals together and didn't do too much snacking in between. Food, itself, simply was not a focus in our house, and meals were opportunities to sit and be with each other either at the start of or at the end of a busy day. Sure, I can remember my growing brother dumping half a box of sugary cereal in his bowl for breakfast and not thinking about calories or limits; I imagine many of us fell into that trap. But, as I recall, that really was the exception in our house. I came of age thinking that I needed to eat to remain healthy and strong, not that I lived to eat. I recognized when my stomach felt full, and that meant I should stop eating. This is the "magic" that I'd like to impart to those of you who struggle with eating more than you should.

We have a seemingly insatiable national hunger. Instead of concentrating on what we eat and taking enjoyment from eating high quality, delicious, wholesome foods, making the most of the calories we have to "spend" in a day, we tend to focus on trying to get down as much of some food as we can. *Non-fat cookies?! Great! How many can I have? A whole row? I can eat as many of them as I would like-they sure won't make me fat if they are non-fat* (um, not exactly). I know well-educated, rational thinking people who will eat an entire box of Girl Scout cookies if given the opportunity. I have seen people eat a pint of ice cream without giving a thought as to how many calories and how much sugar and fat they are consuming. Americans in today's society are obsessed with how much they can get to eat of something. *Give me more, more, more!* The "All You Can Eat Buffet" is my favorite example of our gluttony. We embrace this idea as if it is a good thing. Do yourself a favor, the next time you see an "All you can eat" sign (it really is a disgusting concept when you think about it) translate it as "All The Weight You Can Gain" because any amount of food that you eat beyond what your body requires will only serve to put on the pounds. *Hey, what a bargain!*

We have to stop thinking in terms of being able to eat a lot of anything. We simply cannot do that. Our bodies are not intended to ingest large amounts of food. Most of us do not need to gorge on food now to prepare for a barren winter when food will not be readily available. The psychological reasons behind why we eat when we are not hungry certainly can fill another book, but that is not my focus. I want to help you to reason the way I do, when it comes to food, because it works. I have had to slightly adjust the amount of food that I eat as I got into my 30s and 40s and certainly I have had to increase the amount I exercise, but I have managed to avoid middle-age spread and feel more fit and healthy than ever before.

I do not consider myself to be dieting, on a diet or off a diet or watching my diet. I eat food. I am careful about what goes into my body; it's true, but I never deprive myself of anything I crave or love. I am very mindful about when I eat, what I eat and how much I eat. A good rule of thumb about food is that too much of anything is too much. You can eat too much fruit. You can eat too much "fat-free" candy like jellybeans. You certainly can eat too much cheese (this is one of my areas of struggle). There is no food that you can eat as much of as you would like. That is just the way it is, so forget about that dream. But the good news is that you can enjoy a variety of foods that you love. You do not have to avoid "bad" foods altogether.

Now let us get another thing straight. I do not believe in bad foods vs. good foods. I think it is dangerous to label foods and then to be misled into thinking you can have tons and tons of the "good" foods. How many times have you heard someone say: *It's fruit! Fruit is healthy!* And then proceed to eat 432 grapes? Sure, some fruits are loaded with vitamins and antioxidants and are healthy in the appropriate portions but they are also high in sugar. *Oh, but it's natural sugar.* Yes, this is true, but... it is still sugar. And too much of it can make you overweight. I realized the other day when purchasing a banana from a street vendor that the banana I was buying was so large that I was certain it would never be considered one serving of fruit. Turns out it was worth 3 servings. [3] This is precisely the kind of thing that I encourage you to be wary of. Knowing that we are instructed to eat a recommended 3-5 servings of fruit daily, if I ate that whole banana, I probably would be done for the day with fruit. As you will read later, you would probably not catch me eating a banana that size in one sitting because chances are it would be too filling

---

[3] When I refer to servings in this book please note that I am using the RDA guidelines for a person with a 2000 calorie per day diet.

unless it is my only snack of the day or I'm hiking or doing some activity that requires additional calories.

I am getting hungry writing about food. I am going to have a glass of cold rooibos tea that I have prepared plain, no sugar, and see if that can keep me another half an hour until I make dinner. *A drink? Yes!* Sometimes, we are just thirsty and it seems we are hungry so we reach for a snack. I usually try to drink something first and see if that doesn't tide me over for a bit.

Ok, so I open the fridge and decide a small handful of walnuts and a few raisins will not kill me. I am having that in addition to the tea. When I say a small handful, I mean about 5 or 6 walnut halves and no more raisins then those that could fit on a silver dollar. A tiny snack.

Getting back to good foods vs. bad foods. I read a wonderful book by Michael Pollan called "In Defense of Food". His work is one of the many reasons I was inspired to write this book. He states his guidelines for eating simply on page one: "Eat food. Not too much. Mostly plants". [4] Brilliant. Pollan describes how over the past decades, in the United States, we have gotten away from eating the more traditional, whole, pure foods that our ancestors ate, and we have become accustomed rather to eating convenient, packaged, processed foods that bear little resemblance to anything that comes out of the ground. If you eat mostly foods that are in their original forms, like apples, you tend to do better both from a getting your vitamins and minerals standpoint and also from a feeling satisfied position. I feel less satisfied after eating three Oreo cookies than I do after eating an apple. Why is that? An apple has fiber and vitamins that my body needs in addition to the sugar it provides. The cookies also have sugar, true, and

---

[4] From "In Defense of Food" by Michael Pollan, 2008

provide a very quick and short-lasting source of energy, but that's about it. They have some refined sources of carbohydrates, a little unhealthy fat and nothing much else that I need, so my body is left wanting MORE. The cookies will make me want to eat more even after I have already consumed those empty calories so now I will need more calories in the form of something satisfying. It is a vicious cycle. This is why people feel the need to snack all day long. They are often eating things that do not give their bodies the nutrients they need so their bodies yell that they are hungry even though they have had more than enough calories. The apple, on the other hand, gives us sugar, yes, but also vitamin C, B-complex vitamins, beta-carotene, antioxidants and dietary fiber, so the body processes it more slowly.

Ok, it's time for a dinner break. I am in the mood for pasta, which is high in calories (4 oz of plain whole wheat pasta has 360 calories) and carbohydrates so I want to make the most of my meal and keep the caloric intake down. I have changed the way I eat pasta of late. I make the dish more about the other things in the bowl rather than the pasta itself. I cook ½ the amount of pasta I used to eat, so about 200 calories worth (imagine half a cereal bowl), and today, I am filling the bowl with lightly sautéed spinach, tomato puree, olive oil and a little salt and pepper. It's tasty, nutrient-dense with the spinach and cooked tomatoes, and there's a little healthy fat in the olive oil (I used one tablespoon).

Tonight I have the control of preparing my own meal, but let us say that I am out with friends at a restaurant and we are eating family style. Large platters of pasta, salad, meats and, of course, bread are served. What do I do? Easy. I fill my plate probably ¾ full with salad, take a tiny piece of the meat that is offered, no more than the size of one of my fists, probably even a little less, take a few spoons of the pasta dish and skip the bread. Yes, you heard me, skip the bread. Or, if I must have the bread because it is really warm and fresh and smells heavenly, I take one or two *small* pieces, just to enjoy a little. If it's a long, thin sliced baguette, then I'm talking a slice not more than ½" or 1" thick. And I might even put a tiny bit of butter on it (more on butter and fats later). And when dessert comes, what do I do? Well, for starters, I never order one whole dessert for myself anymore unless someone has a gun to my head. And even then, I would probably ask the gun holder if he/she would share the dessert with me. For who has decided what a portion of this delicate chocolate ganache should be? The chef? The manager? Neither knows me or my body or what my caloric intake should be. And they are probably giving me a piece the size of my head, unless we are in a trendy little Manhattan restaurant where they serve a sliver no bigger than a pinky finger. Even then I might split it.

Desserts are wonderful. They are my favorite part of any meal. I have learned that I do not need to eat much of them to get the satisfaction of having had something truly decadent. Don't think: How am I going to fill up my gut? Do think: Have I given my body the nutrients and calories it needs? This shift will have you on the road to mindful eating. You will think, Hmmm... that was a satisfying meal and I don't feel hunger, so chances are my body does not really need any more food. If you want a little decadence, then a bite or two of something can really be enough. You can have your cake and avoid the guilt. I was out for dinner a few weeks ago with some good friends and the FOUR of us split a modest-sized piece of cake. And no one left crying.

When I have spent time in Europe, I have noticed that both in restaurants and homes Europeans often serve a small amount of fruit after the meal, to cleanse the palette. I love this practice and try to do it when I can at home. I will have a couple slices of a pear or an apple or some berries. That helps also to satisfy my need for a little sugar and then I have an even smaller amount of something decadent. It is all about making the most caloric or fattening thing the *smallest* part of your meal. So while you don't have to do away with the things you crave, you can learn to enjoy them in lesser quantities.

Again, this book is not so much about what not to eat as it is about helping you to decide what to eat, how much to eat and how to eat. This is where we have gone astray. We eat much more than our bodies need, and the result, of course, is obesity. If we constantly fight urges to fill up on foods that are unhealthy and then find ourselves binging on those very same foods that we have labeled as "the enemy, something is wrong with our innate sense that tells us what we need. We used to have a built-in monitor to tell us when to stop eating. Somewhere along the evolutionary line, we have lost that valuable switch. Despite the daily onslaught of "all you can eat" advertisements, I have taught myself how to get the monitor back. Very little throws me dangerously off course where I feel that I've blown it. Not a party, not the holidays, not an urge to bake my whole wheat brownies or Bobby Flay's Chocolate Chip Cookie recipe with two kinds of muscovado sugar and two different chocolates. I would like to help you return to a state where you are more in tune with your body and its nutritional needs and less afraid of eating foods that you love. It's about common sense and balance.

KAREN'S SNACK BOX

1) Late afternoon snack:

> 1 tbspn Trader Joe's crunchy natural pb and
>
> 1 tbspn Polaner all fruit Strawberry preserves on
>
> 2 slices whole grain flax seed bread with 2 stalks of cut celery sticks

2) Evening snack:

> Handful of whole-wheat cereal squares, a handful of almonds or raw veggies or a handful of walnuts and raisins.
>
> One 12 oz glass plain red rooibos tea

3) Ice cream snack- 1/3 c berries with two tablespoons ice cream

CHAPTER THREE

The Practice of Thanksgiving Non-stuffing

Thanksgiving really is my favorite holiday. I love all of the hoopla, the family, the friends, usually the crisp northeastern weather, the turkey and stuffing, the fresh cranberries, the desserts. I love the idea of taking a moment to give thanks to those who make our lives worth living. Why not celebrate with a feast?

I just do not know when the word "feast" came to be synonymous with gorging ourselves until our pants need to be unzipped. Why can't we have a celebration with food where the feast is about the variety of the wonderful dishes that everyone prepares and brings, not the amount of each of these items we manage to ram into our throats? Again, as with the "All you can eat" buffet, this is a pretty senseless tradition. Here are some statements often overheard at Thanksgiving gatherings or shortly thereafter:

"Oh my God, I ate so much I feel sick."

"I had to have three helpings of the stuffing, it was so good!"

" I gained at least 10 lbs over the holidays

" I was so stuffed I couldn't button my jeans!"

"If I never eat another meal, I think I'll be just fine."

"I feel like a fat pig."

"I can't wait for the leftovers

"I better hit the gym tomorrow…"

Honestly, of all of the above, the one about leftovers I mind the least, because it at least shows some restraint. I am assuming that if there are indeed leftovers, that someone realized it was time to stop eating! I wish everyone would stop and think when reaching for that third helping of sweet potato pie, that they can always ask to take some home with them, if the feast is not at their home. If you are by chance the host, well then, just put a little bit aside for you and slip it into the fridge. No need to eat everything all at once. This is, for the time being, no longer the depression era. We usually do know where our next meal is coming from.

About 10 years ago, I decided I no longer wanted to have that too full feeling at the end of the Thanksgiving meal. I didn't like the way it felt to have a bulging tummy that ached. Fancy that. I made up my mind, then and there, not to ever again feel uncomfortable after eating. I came to the realization that I could only comfortably eat a small amount of food at Thanksgiving (or any meal for that matter). That meant that if I wanted to sample most of the things that were presented to me, I had to be smart. I had to take very small portions of the offerings, so that I could enjoy everything and yet not develop a bellyache. And with wanting to save room for desserts, this meant I had to be even more careful. And what did I learn? It was much more enjoyable to sample the different dishes and not feel gross afterward than it had been previously to heap things on my plate and eat hundreds and hundreds of calories more than I normally did in a day.

Now, when I sit down to a Thanksgiving meal, I take the dinner plate and don't expect to pack it more full with food than I do at a regular meal. I alter the amounts of the items I'm taking, and if the side dishes are enticing then I know I have to eat less turkey than I might otherwise choose to. I take a spoonful of this, of that; try to keep the veggie portions larger than the starches, and I always go easy on sauces and gravy. I take just a dab for flavor. I also try to start out my Thanksgiving Day with a strong workout if possible, just to kick-start my metabolism and give myself a reason to need a few more calories.

Ok, interruption. Talking about Thanksgiving is making me hungry for lunch. As I write this sentence, I tell myself I am starving. I really want cheese. I am going to chop up some endive, beefsteak tomato, celery and lettuce. I've now put a little extra virgin olive oil and red wine vinegar (about one tablespoon total) on my salad and mixed it up in a bowl with a dash of salt and pepper. I have some delicious extra sharp cheddar cheese that I must have, so I will take a one ounce square of it –that's not very much but it's quite fatty-has about 30% of the Daily Value (DV)[5] for saturated fat just in that square alone-and eat that with my salad. I want some more protein and don't want to rely only on the fatty cheese, so I'll heat up a half of a leftover baked lemon chicken cutlet from last night's dinner. I also have a hankering for a few potato chips so I'm taking 5 or 6 large Kettle lightly salted chips (not half a bag) and I am

---

[5] The recommended daily value is for a person eating an average 2,000 calorie diet.

enjoying them as well. Especially when I am eating alone, I like to be in the practice of taking items out of their containers, putting them on my plate, and then putting the bag or box away, so I am not tempted to add to what I have already taken. This helps me to control my portions. I do this also when I pack snacks for the road. I prefer to pack just the amount I want to eat for the day, rather than take an entire bag of cookies or chips with me and just hope for the best.

I am drinking water, plain water. No soda, no beer, no wine, no juice. This isn't a big sacrifice for me, because I don't like beer, don't like sugary soda many times, juice and wine is too acidic for my tummy. Except for diet soda, all of the aforementioned items will add calories to my diet that I am happy to pass up so I can eat more food. I figure since my body needs water and it does not really need the other drinks, it's probably best to drink water whenever I can. I'm not saying I never enjoy a diet soda, a glass of wine, a cocktail, or a decaf coffee with a little half and half and sugar, but in general, I prefer to drink water or a plain tea with some natural sweetness to it like rooibos. It allows me to have more calories available to "spend" on food and I find it much more satisfying to eat rather than to drink. It's a personal choice. Keep in mind though, that if you are drinking something highly caloric that does not have the nutrients your body requires, it will be the same as eating a hunk of white bread. You are getting calories, but practically no nutrients, so your body will still be telling you it's hungry and will beckon you to eat. Feed me, Seymour.

Back to Thanksgiving and portion control. I would like to be a captain for the Portion Police. I think that would be a fantastic job. Thanksgiving, of course, would be my biggest day of the year. I would go from holiday gathering to holiday gathering, whispering quietly into the ear of Uncle Morty, about to loosen his belt buckle in order to allow for another slice of Aunt Mona's pumpkin pie. I'd say, "Really Morty? Do you want to be that guy? Why today, in this moment, do you need another piece of pie? I am going to wrap a piece up for you to take home, ok? You have had plenty already, my friend." And in my fantasy, Uncle Morty would be appreciative and thank me for my efforts to save him discomfort and way too many calories.

Obviously, I am not this annoying in real life with my friends (at least I don't think I am), but I do hope that I model good behavior. For instance, a few weeks ago I was at a Yankee game and went to the hotdog stand to buy a kosher frank, one of my non-guilty indulgences at a ballgame. I was upset to learn that they were out of the regular sized franks and they could only offer me a foot long dog. Well of course I bought the foot long dog. I can't go to a ballgame and not have a ballpark frank.

I try not to be wasteful. There are times when I know that something is just too much for me and I will offer it to a friend or bring it home or if that's not possible then I will sometimes discard it if all options are exhausted, rather than eat something that I don't wish to eat. When I got back to my seat with the foot long dog, I had every intention of giving it my best shot, but I thought the bun would put me over the edge. That's a lot of bread, a lot of white bread. My friend also purchased the foot longer and I did not want to make her feel bad about eating the entire dog, bun and all. I ate the bun with the first half of the dog and then left the rest of the bun behind while I tried to eat the rest of the dog, figuring that with all of the other disturbing ingredients one hears are in hotdogs, there is at least some protein there. I must say I thoroughly enjoyed that dog. No guilt. I am not into food shaming. I do want to feel that I'm doing my best to eat nutrient-dense, healthful foods but when I'm faced with a situation where I am going to eat something that's not considered to be healthy, I eat with moderation and good sense. It should be noted that I did not consume beers that night, cotton candy, Crackerjacks or any of the other fare offered at the stadium. I had my kosher frank and did not feel disgusted with myself. And on that particular night, I did not even require the antacid that I always bring to chase the dog with, just in case.

Our idea of what constitutes a reasonable portion of food can easily become skewed at a salad bar. I work in a hospital that has a cafeteria with a fresh and well- priced salad bar. I am fortunate. I am also fortunate in that I realize how much salad I should be taking. The rather large plastic "to-go"containers can hold pounds of salad, but it does not mean I should fill mine up with as much as it will hold. I am not proud to say that it took me years to recognize that the fact that I was throwing out so much salad after my meal meant I was taking too much. Now I have a more accurate sense of how much I will eat and just because it is salad does not mean we should overload on it. Too much nutritious food is still too much food. You CAN eat too much healthy food.

The other day, I was perusing the salad bar and taking a little of this a little of that and, of course, at the end I was drawn to the cheese. Always the cheese. This particular day they had cubes of provolone. Yum. I took the tongs provided and picked out 4 or 5 small pieces of cheese, enough to make approximately an ounce or so, give or take. I noticed the woman next to me had sprinkled her mound of salad with probably 25 pieces of cheese. Now, knowing what I know about the DV of saturated fat for a regular fat cheese, that lady had well over the daily value for saturated fat in cheese alone, for any sized person. Not to mention the loads of creamy dressing she had poured over her salad. She was probably thinking, wow, I had a big healthy salad for lunch. I can be more lenient with my dinner and allow for pasta, dessert and a couple glasses of wine. She had already had more than enough fat for her body by 2 pm and she likely was not aware of this fact or the consequences of eating more fat and calories than her body needs.

I try to be aware of what I put into my body and the ramifications of eating more food than my frame can handle. As it turns out, I can only take two or three cupfuls of salad. As healthy as it is to get all of those green and red vegetables, my body doesn't need more than that and my stomach feels too full when I overdo it. You may be able to eat more than I can without feeling uncomfortable. I have spent so many afternoons thinking why on earth have I stuffed myself with salad? Nowadays I take about ½ the salad I used to take and waste. And I finish every bite.

When it comes to what I take at the salad bar, I usually try to take most of the salad greens and reds and oranges. Then I might take a little protein like black beans or grilled chicken strips and about an ounce of cheese. Sometimes the bar offers quinoa or barley salads and I will take a small amount of those too, knowing that they usually are made with oil and I want to make sure I'm not getting too much hidden fat. I will almost always top my salad with a spoon of extra virgin olive oil and either balsamic or red wine vinegar or sometimes lemon juice. I never go for creamy dressings-again, I figure since I really don't prefer them anyhow, why use my calories and fat there? I like to save my fat for my Achilles' heel, CHOCOLATE.

Chocolate is my favorite thing to eat in the entire world; has been for years. I am pretty picky about my chocolate-I only like dark. It doesn't have to be 80% cacao, even 65% is fine, but I really can't say that milk chocolate does much of anything for me. I can pass on a Hershey bar or a Nestle's crunch anytime, but put a Mounds in front of me and I'm in heaven. Chocolate, as we all know, is fattening. While much has been written about dark chocolate over the past few years and its ability to lower blood pressure and LDL (bad cholesterol), the helpful antioxidants and flavonoids, the good news always comes with an important caveat about eating it in moderation. The higher you go with the cacao content, the less sugar there is in the chocolate, but the higher the saturated fat content. As chocolate is my favorite food and one I am quite certain could sustain me endlessly if need be, I choose to eat a little of it everyday. Yes, everyday. Here's where I think a little psychology comes into play: because I am eating some everyday, I never feel deprived, never feel there is this one amazing food that I cannot have. And because I know I am going to have some again tomorrow, I don't feel like I need lots and lots of it. When I do enjoy some, I really and truly appreciate this perfect food. I respect this delectable treat that is dark chocolate, but I do not abuse it.

And what about the quality of the chocolate I eat? Since it's my favorite indulgence, I want it to be really, really GOOD chocolate. I don't want to waste my time with second-rate crappy stuff. Find the best of whatever it is you love and savor it. You'll feel like you're being good to yourself, and that is a wonderful thing that we all deserve. We should thoroughly enjoy the foods we love and not feel guilty about eating them.

How do I go about eating an appropriate portion? From what I've learned, it seems that one ounce of dark chocolate daily is enough to give a person the heart healthy benefits. One ounce is not as much as most of us would like to think it is. Remember the size of a Chunky candy bar, that little square chunk of four smaller squares? That is 1.4 ounces, so an ounce would be about 2/3 of a Chunky. If I want to keep my dark chocolate intake reasonable, so that I can enjoy it every day, then I need to give some thought to how much I am eating. I cannot just eat it indiscriminately. A one-ounce portion of dark chocolate, depending on the cocoa content, can have 30% or higher of suggested saturated fat for the day. Some days I feel I need almost the whole amount at once. That might be the kind of day I'm having. On other days, I have a few bites here and there throughout the day to make it last. Sometimes I like to eat some dark chocolate with a handful of walnuts. I find it to be a very energetic and satisfying snack, especially before the gym. And I get more good fats including omega 3 fatty acids with the walnuts, but those must be eaten with restraint as well.

When I go to the movies, I like to enjoy some Junior Mints as my movie candy. Might I point out that Europeans don't feel the need to snack at the movies? They go to the movies to watch films. Fancy that. This box of Junior Mints that I buy for $5 or so, unless I've had the foresight to go to the drugstore and get a box for $2, has more sugar and fat than I want. It's a rather large box. Still not worth $5, but that's another issue. I think it contains 2 ½ servings in one box. Although Junior Mints and Peppermint Patties are sometimes referred to as "low fat" candy, they still have fat and they still have lots and lots of sugar. Unless someone is sharing them with me, I stop myself before I've eaten too many and I take them home and save them. My trick is that I pour just a few at a time into my hand and then I close the box and put it away or in the little cup holder on my armrest. I don't leave the box open and don't leave my hand continuously in the box, the way some people do with popcorn. Just because you want to enjoy some candy at the movies does not mean you have to destroy your healthy eating habits. Have a little and then save the rest. Put them in your bag. No need to make a pig of yourself. Pretend you're European and you're just there to watch the film. You'll seem very classy.

Nuts. Let's talk about nuts. What a great snack- protein, fiber, some with very healthy fats, very few carbohydrates. My favorites are walnuts and almonds. I always have them on hand at work and I bring them in little packets with me when I travel. Although they do have some good fats, they also can make you fat. A handful is all you should have for the day. That's not a lot of nuts, people. Since I love to have them at work, I portion out about 5 days worth in a small Tupperware container and bring those with me on a Monday so I have them for the week. It makes more sense to me than to bring an entire bag and hope that I can keep track of how much I eat. Why set myself up for failure? If I have already pre-portioned snacks then I avoid the temptation to overdo it. There's not a danger of getting carried away and forgetting how much I've eaten while I'm working or talking on the phone. If I've eaten more than half the container of nuts and it's Tuesday afternoon, then I know I've got to find some other snacks that are less caloric and less fatty to keep me going. This is precisely why I like having fresh fruits and vegetables, in particular, on hand.

I know some people are fond of eating out of the bag or box, especially while watching television or a movie, BUT... yes this is a very big but, it is extremely unwise and I discourage you from doing so. You can really lose control over how much you are eating. You grab the bag of chips, or the box of popcorn or the Milk duds, and you munch during the film and you have no idea how much sugar or fat or calories you are eating and you probably don't care. *I'm at the movies, it doesn't count*. Yes, I've actually heard that. In regard to this behavior at home, I say, make yourself wash an extra plate and put the food you want on a plate or in a bowl. Is it really worth all of those extra calories that you probably don't need, to save yourself washing that dish? See how much you are eating, visually appreciate it, and it will inevitably mean more to you than downing a bag of chips.

Chips. I love chips. Here's what I do with chips. I never make chips my one snack. If I feel like some chips, I take a few out of the bag, maybe 4 or 5 really big ones, and I put them on the side of my plate. If I'm having a salad, I'll eat a few chips with my salad. I'm eating mostly salad, but I'm also enjoying some of the salty crunchy chips that I adore. My latest favorites? Kettle brand sour cream and cheddar. I take them out of the bag and put the bag away so I'm not eating chips mindlessly out of the bag. I'm still having some chips and loving them. And I try to make them last throughout my salad so I'm not missing them at the end and craving more. This is another tactic I use that I believe helps: pace.

When I'm at the movies eating Milk duds or Junior Mints, I offer some to my movie date or the friends that I'm with. If they say yes, wonderful-instant calorie reduction. If they say no, then I have to make sure that I don't eat the entire box before the previews even end. One really should not eat the entire box even during the course of the movie. It's too much sugar and empty calories for one person. Eat candy sparingly. It's candy, not a whole grain cereal. It has very little nutritional value and it is not your friend, even though its taste might tell you otherwise. Please, I'm the first person to wish that York Peppermint Patties were their own food group and that we were supposed to eat 5 servings of a day. We have to get used to treating treats as just that, treats. Candy is not a food group and I doubt that it ever will be. Even when certain candy is marked as a "low fat food", it does not mean you can eat it all day long without getting fat. Low fat foods can still make you fat. Jellybeans have no fat but are loaded with sugar that can most definitely make you fat. While I do not encourage you to view certain foods as forbidden, I want you to respect food and have an understanding of what constitutes good nutrition and giving your body what it needs. Once you concentrate on sensible eating habits that are providing you with nutrients, you won't have much room for empty calorie snacks and you will find it easier to eat them sparingly and to appreciate them.

For my part, when I'm left with the box of candy that no one wants to share with me, I limit myself to a few handfuls during the show. I'll often take the rest home and put it in the fridge for some other movie at a later date, maybe something I've DVR'd on Turner Classics. Who says that I have to eat every piece of candy in the box in one sitting? Does it somehow lessen my movie-going experience if I take some candy home with me? I've even taken to sometimes buying just the regular size candy box at the drug store before going to the movies, to ensure that I won't have a giant box at my disposal. It's also quite a bit more economical. Then, if I really feel the need to eat the entire box, I have more of a sense of how much I am eating and how many calories and sugars I'm getting and of course, it's a smaller, more reasonable portion to be eating. You can read more about my snacking tips in Chapter Eight.

Portion control is within your grasp. There is no reason for you to feel at the mercy of restaurants, friends, supermarkets and vendors who prepare foods in unrealistic portions that are significantly more than you want to consume. While you are bound to find yourself in situations where food is being served to you in large quantities, i.e. Thanksgiving, you can find ways to avoid eating more than you need to eat without insulting the host or wasting food. And generally, saving some of what you have now for later helps out your wallet in the long run. I almost always have lunch for the next day after I've had a meal out. It saves me time, money and calories. Win, win, and win.

KAREN'S LUNCH BOX

Lunch:

1) Salad- endive, lettuce, beefsteak tomato, olive oil and vinegar, salt and pepper

2) 1 oz sharp cheddar cheese

3) A handful of kettle chips

4) Half a small baked lemon chicken cutlet (half the size of my open hand)

5) Water

CHAPTER FOUR

You Say Diet, I Say Eat It

I do not intend to endorse any one diet in this book. I don't subscribe to the idea of "dieting", meaning to eat a special course of food in order to restrict oneself and omit certain foods. I usually eat whatever I feel like eating. The caveat here is that I have conditioned myself over the years to eat generally quite healthy foods and, even more important, perhaps, is that I control HOW MUCH of the foods I love that I eat.

I cannot tell you how many times in my life I have heard friends and acquaintances say they are going on a diet. If you are a middle-aged adult and you can't control your weight through your ups and downs of dieting on and off, chances are that the next diet on which you are about to embark is not going to the do the trick either. Why not? Because you haven't yet conditioned yourself to believe that food is your friend. Food provides you with life-sustaining nutrients and certain foods are so delectable that we derive pleasure from eating them. Food can make us very happy and if we control what we eat instead of the food controlling us, we can enjoy eating and not feel deprived by our choices. Let's start by getting rid of the idea of bad foods versus good foods.

I don't believe that eating any one food causes people to have trouble maintaining their weight. Lately, I've been noticing ads popping up on my computer stating "Five foods NEVER to eat!!" There is a place in any healthy, balanced diet for the much-maligned carbohydrates, for example, or for red meat, or for sweets. But any of these items eaten in excess will most certainly cause problems in regard to weight maintenance and also our general health. When diets warn us to stay away from carbohydrates, the thing to keep in mind is that yes, in the present proportion and forms that carbohydrates occur in the American diet, carbohydrates can be troublesome. But eaten in moderation, complex carbohydrates can be tolerated and do have value.

Remember that our cave ancestors did not have bread and pastries. They ate a lot of meat. They killed animals and ate the meat when they were hungry and they did not sit around watching television or staring at their computers and iphones. They did not have cupboards filled with stored food nor did they graze. They ate when they were hungry. And when they were hungry, they ate meat and plants in their purest forms. Just because we decided that it's convenient and tasty to have all of the processed cereals and breads and packaged foods that we now have, does not mean that our bodies were intended to be fed this way. We got smart, or so we thought, and we invented easier ways of doing things and I love having the ability to go pick up a loaf of bread at the market but it doesn't mean that that item is the best thing for me. I find it hard to believe that meat is unhealthy (while I do understand people not wanting to eat it because they don't want animals to be killed) when, originally, it was a major component of the human diet. I think that good and bad foods exist only in relation to how much we include them in our diets and in what forms.

I sometimes keep a little container of cookies with me at my desk in the office. It usually has one or two organic cookies in there or perhaps something I've baked myself, like the chocolate chip cookie recipe I've included at the end of Chapter Five. I like to have a cookie with my morning tea when I get into work. My coworkers inevitably walk into my office and see me dipping a cookie into my tea at 9:30 am and are aghast. "Cookies this early?! My, aren't you decadent!" Really? First off, cookies are perfect for dunking in tea or coffee or a cold glass of milk. Secondly, back off. What's wrong with cookies? Or brownies for that matter? Yes, sometimes I dunk a small brownie in my tea. The point is, it gives me pleasure! Am I hurting anyone?

Now let's put my morning cookie into some context. If two hours earlier, I have had a breakfast of a sugarless wholegrain cereal, some berries and a little low fat milk or yogurt, then what's the harm in my dunking one small cookie into a cup of plain tea? Am I really that decadent? People think nothing about downing a large chocolate croissant for breakfast which is not nearly as nutrient-dense or low fat as the breakfast I have described, but they think of a croissant as a breakfast food, whereas cookies are not to be eaten before noon. They also think nothing of letting their children have breakfast cereals loaded with refined sugar. Think about my choice, though; it makes me happy, it's a small, reasonable portion, and I have already had a healthy breakfast. I'm not having cookies in place of my breakfast. Cookies are not a bad food. No shame in having a cookie now and again. It's better to have one, out in the open, as I did, than to sneak a row of Nutter Butters from your desk drawer throughout the day, is it not?

We have got to rid ourselves of the idea that foods are inherently bad. Well, ok, certain foods really ARE bad, such as things made with lots of trans-fatty acids, but frankly, at that point, we are not really talking about food anymore. I dare not call an item laden with partially hydrogenated oils, "food"; it's more of a food substitute by the time it gets that refined and far removed from what comes out of the ground. But I really do want to impart to you that there is actually a place for most foods in your diet. To think of some as bad and some as good doesn't serve you as well as considering what value the different foods hold for you and making your decisions accordingly.

It's time for lunch though, so I need to eat. It is a hot summer day and I can't think of eating a big meal but, at present, I feel as though I'm starving. I'm going to have what I call "things" today. It's where I take a plate out of the cabinet and then pretend I'm at a party and I'm taking little bits of this and that and put them on the plate, like hors d'oeuvres. I have celery sticks, a handful of baby carrots, a Belgian endive, a palmful of walnuts, a small piece of Gouda cheese (1 oz square) and three small slices of salami. I also was in the mood for a dill pickle so I took one slice of a pickle as well. Now, some might say salami is fatty and not a healthy food. Well, if I eat 15 pieces of it on a pizza or eat half of the salami itself then yes, it probably isn't the most healthful choice, but as I have practiced discretion and have taken just three small pieces (a bit thicker than what you'd see on a pizza, maybe ¼ inch thick) it's not such a bad thing. And we've got some protein here. I have fat in the cheese, the salami and the walnuts (good fats too, here). These are the smallest parts of my plate. The bulk of what I'm eating is carrots and celery and endive. When I eat this way, it's also nice because I don't feel obliged to dress my vegetables, since I'm having tasty cheese and salami at the same time as the raw veggies, so I am not having the extra calories and fat that dressing might hold. As usual, I want a little something sweet after I eat, so I'm having half of an orange and a small piece (1/3 oz.) of bittersweet dark chocolate.

Back to good foods versus bad foods. As you can see, my philosophy is that I eat what I want but with a conscience and a context. When a person at a birthday party says, " I don't eat cake" or "I can't have cake", I feel for them. I want everyone (barring those who have health restrictions like diabetics) to be able to have at least a small piece of birthday cake. I know a man who is convinced that he simply can never, under any circumstances, have sugar. Now, he can have the natural sugar that is in fruits but he does not eat anything with added sugar and most things with flour either. He does not have the self-control to eat these items in small amounts and is convinced that they make him fat. If he has even a bite it might trigger a binge. He has had years of therapy and has been diagnosed with an eating disorder and thus he makes sure to avoid certain foods that he considers "dangerous". While I agree that he probably should stay clear of foods that he cannot eat in reasonably sized portions, I would disagree that the foods in and of themselves, are inherently bad or unhealthy.

I would like to propose that instead of ganging up on the "bad" foods, we think of them as foods that we should pay some attention to while enjoying them, so that we don't over do them. I want us to have a realistic idea of how to enjoy that piece of birthday cake without feeling guilty, sick or just plain disappointed in ourselves for having given in to temptation. Birthday cake is generally loaded with refined sugar and is quite sweet. One doesn't need a lot of birthday cake to feel she has had this sugary delight. I tend to ask for a smaller piece and then take a few bites and leave most of the frosting behind. Or I'll ask another party guest to split a piece with me. Most people like that option and are pleased that you gave them the opportunity to opt out of a larger slice. An entire piece of birthday cake, (I am referring to a frosted layer cake) or the size that they give you in a typical American diner, will actually add hundreds and hundreds of calories to your daily diet and should not be a regular part of anyone's diet in that quantity. Still, I would be hard pressed to call cake a bad food. Is it the most nutritious food? No. Is it filled with empty calories? Yes indeed. But, eaten in small amounts, once in a while, it will not disturb your efforts to eat a balanced diet and avoid weight gain.

In the event you've eaten a piece of cake that is larger than what you had intended, all is not lost. You have not "blown your diet" with the evil cake. If I could not resist that rather large piece of homemade chocolate layer cake that my coworker made for the 3:30 pm office party, I would make adjustments with my eating for the remainder of the day. I would be mindful that I ate an entire piece of cake and that my body is now requiring less calories to maintain my weight but still needs nutrition. I might just have a small salad for dinner, with no cheese or added fat other than a couple teaspoons of olive oil, and maybe just a little lean protein like turkey. No pasta, no bread, no refined carbohydrates. Veggies and protein is the way I would balance that afternoon cake. I'd limit my sugars since I've already had plenty and then give my body what it has to be craving-vitamins and minerals. It is all about balance, it is not about you can eat this and you cannot eat that. Another one of my rules of thumb is that if it's not real food (and cake is not real food, my friends) then it should be eaten in small amounts. You can't go wrong. And if you're not sure, it's probably not real food.

On the other side of the coin, let's take a perceived "good" food and examine it, shall we? Let's take almonds. I love almonds. High in fiber, almonds have protein, lots of heart-healthy monounsaturated fats[6] and whole almonds, which include the skins, also contain flavonoids, a helpful antioxidant. Great. Almonds are a healthy snack, agreed. Here's how a healthy food can throw you off course if you are not mindful, though. If you sit down with a 16 oz bag of almonds and eat say, half the bag, thinking you're being virtuous by not eating the whole thing, you've eaten 1280 calories and over 200% of your total fat allowance for the day.[7] For someone small like

---

[6] Monounsaturated fats have been shown to reduce levels of LDL in the blood.

[7] This is based on the nutritional information listed for a 16oz bag of Trader Joe's raw almonds.

me, that's 75% of my calories for the day. I can't snack on almonds like that. Sure they are healthy, but only when eaten in moderation. That 16 oz bag contains 16 servings of nuts. That's why when I eat nuts, I think about what will fit in the palm of my hand. If you're 5'9", 160 lbs, then the palm of your hand will be bigger than mine and you can eat more. If I eat nuts with abandon, then I won't have room in my body for other things that I also need to be eating. Again, it's all about balance.

When I'm in Starbucks and I want a cool drink, I do not have a frappuccino or some fancy coffee topped with whipped cream and sugary syrups that's got 1,000 calories and goodness knows how much fat. The latest craze is the pumpkin latte. I am, instead, enjoying an iced decaf coffee with a splash of half and half. That's my fun, the half and half. Makes it creamy and I can't bear a cup of coffee with that lame, muddy color that it becomes with non-fat milk. Watery brown. It's so much more enjoyable for me to have half and half so I have a little of it and enjoy every sip. As for sugar… I don't pooh pooh sugar as much as some. I know that lots of added sugar is not my friend, but again, if I have a coffee drink once in a while then I want to have it the way I will most enjoy it. I usually add 1 or 2 sugar packets, raw if they have it, and I never use imitation sugars because they actually taste too sweet for my liking and I'd rather have a little of the real thing than its imitation.

Back to real food vs. fake food. I do find it helpful to plan my meals and snacks considering real vs. fake food. If I can build my meals primarily from real food than I can throw in some less real food that has been processed if it's that important to me. As long as most of what I consume is whole food that is fairly natural, then I ease up on my enjoyment of a fake snack here or there. I never think of any food as "bad" as long as it hasn't been processed too much. I tell myself that in order to enjoy this food I must do so in moderation.

The more I learn to enjoy more natural foods, the less I crave processed things.

Some years back, I tried for a time to go completely without refined sugar. I did it for a couple of weeks. It was tough to kick the habit at first, and as with any addiction, I went through a difficult period of withdrawal. Once I was off the stuff, however, I felt pretty good. I had fewer ups and downs throughout the day and found my level of energy more evenly paced. I somehow felt "cleaner", whether that was my imagination or not, I do not know. I even recall my skin being clearer. It was a difficult couple of weeks. There are so many foods that are staples in my diet that have added sugar. And I love those foods-cereal, cookies, ice cream. I made every effort to make this no sugar thing work and I do think that I felt better during the "diet". Sugar can wreak quite a lot of havoc on our bodies and one of the issues we read more and more about these days is overall inflammation caused by too much sugar. It can affect everything from our joints to our arteries.

As much as I eventually enjoyed that feeling of not eating sugar, I began to miss certain foods and certainly could not continue without eating dark chocolate. Having experienced that sugar-free feeling, I was not so sure I wanted to go back to full-throttle sugar consumption and knew I had to reach some kind of compromise. Also, I noticed during the sugar-free period, it was much easier for me to have a flatter stomach and there was less stuff around my mid-section in general. Oh, I want to add this, too: The other day at work, someone commented to me that I should go ahead and have that piece of angel food cake because it has no fat. I said to this person, make no mistake, if there is in fact no fat in the cake it does not mean it will not make one fat. Sugar, even though it has no fat in and of itself, gets stored as fat in the body. People love to hide behind that "fat-free" phrase. I did end up having a small taste of the angel food cake. But I did so in a very educated way, knowing full well that a few bites would suffice.

When it came time to add back the sugary foods that I had been missing, I tried to do so with some new knowledge under my belt. Since living without sugar really did make me feel better, perhaps I had been eating too much of it and I should be more wary of the added sugar in my diet. I should try to eat sugar moderately. Not deprive myself of it, but eat it mindfully. If you respect your body and your health then you will most likely be eating in this way already. For example, I paid more attention to the cereals I chose. I switched to more whole grain cereals that contained little if any added sugar and perhaps some spice like cinnamon, which gave it sweetness naturally.

I have also learned to enjoy the natural sugars in foods like bananas and often top them with the yummy taste of a little natural peanut butter with no added sugar. I found that the sugar in the banana was sweet enough to get me used to eating natural peanut butter. To date, that is one of my favorite snacks. When I saw how much added sugar was in juices, cookies, and frozen desserts like ice cream, I made a concerted effort to change my eating habits where those items were concerned. I don't do away with them in total (although juices I have no problem omitting), but instead of eating a bowl of ice cream; I learned to enjoy a few spoonfuls. Instead of pouring myself a full glass of juice, I might pour a glass of water and then just add a splash of juice to flavor it. If I want to enjoy a fruit, then I think it's usually best to get the fiber from the fruit in its original state, like cranberries, oranges, or apples, rather than just the sugar and calories from a juice. Again, juice is not a "bad food" (or beverage) but there are smarter ways to enjoy what I like about the juice. Over the many years of my childhood and early adulthood, I became conditioned to tolerate all of the sugar in the foods I previously had been eating. After several years in the opposite direction, my body eventually became used to lesser amounts of sugar and I no longer desire those greater amounts of sugars. I have a lower tolerance now for sweets. This is most definitely something that can be adjusted within us with a little effort. And I'm not driving myself crazy about it. If I feel like eating a Snickers bar (and sometimes I really, really do) then I have the candy bar. But now that I'm more sensitive to sugar again, I usually eat half of it and then feel-ok, that's enough sugar for now. I can save the rest for another time.

I love when people say things to me like "Karen! I would not have thought that you would eat candy or cookies. You seem so healthy." First of all, they must not know me very well, because I rarely travel more than 500 feet without a supply of something sweet on hand. Secondly, I respond to them that there is no reason not to enjoy some treats now and again and that every healthy diet is made up of a balance of the foods needed to keep the body strong and running plus the things that feed our soul. There's this one guy at work that, every time he sees me eating, has to comment that he can't believe I'm eating what I'm eating. "You're eating meat? You're eating chocolate? You're eating lasagna? I thought you were a healthy person. I'm surprised at you." Like I did something wrong or have something to be ashamed of. I want to say "@#$% you!" It gets frustrating after a while. I told him that I eat ice cream almost nightly in the summer, just a spoon or two of Haagen Dazs full fat ice cream. He looked at me in disbelief and added, " If I had ice cream every night, I'd be huge." Not if you ate it mindfully.

The other issue that my interaction with this coworker brings up is that most people want to believe that I starve myself in order to remain trim. I've had women on elevators say: " You must never eat!" "What are you, a size zero?" "I used to be as thin as you and then I had my kids". People assume that because I'm slender and not overweight, there is no harm in commenting on my size. Well here's what I just had for dinner, Elevator Ladies:

I was hankering for some take out Italian food from Tony's, my neighborhood Italian place. I ordered meat ravioli, a salad and a diet caffeine free coke. I try not to drink soda but I really like to have one with Italian food, unless I'm having a nice glass of wine. Or, for me, a half glass, as I get silly drunk on a whole glass. What came in my order was enough ravioli for two or three meals, and a salad for also two or three meals. I received two large hunks of Italian bread, which I promptly tossed in the garbage. I hate to waste food, but as I believe that the only thing the white bread does for me is make me fat, I tossed it. I had a nice amount of salad, which had lettuce, green pepper, grape tomato, red onion, red cabbage and carrots, and I dressed it with their olive oil vinaigrette. The ravioli were huge so I ate only about four and then I felt I had had enough. Did I feel deprived that I left eight more ravioli in the container? No. Why ? I can eat them tomorrow for dinner. I was quite satisfied.

Eating what you love doesn't have to be an exercise in mental torture. With a small amount of effort, you can have what you enjoy and feel good about your decisions. I never ever go to bed thinking either 1) Oh man, I wish I had had that pie today at lunch... OR 2) Oh crap, I really wish I did not have that pie today at lunch. There are so many challenges we all have to face in the day; food does not have to be a source of stress for us.

RECIPE for Sea Salt Brownie Bites

I've adapted an old brownie recipe of mine to include whole-wheat flour and sea salt. I fell in love with Trader Joe's petite brownie bites and wanted to make my own. The small bites allow you to have a little bit of sheer indulgence without overdoing it.

4 oz unsweetened chocolate

1 ½ sticks butter

2 cups organic sugar

1 cup whole-wheat flour

3 large organic eggs

1 tsp pure vanilla

kosher salt (a sprinkle or two)

Melt butter and chocolate over low heat on top of stove in a heavy pot. Stir frequently. Add the other ingredients except for salt. Don't beat -just stir until ingredients are mixed. Pour into greased and floured pan or use cooking spray. Bake @ 350 degrees for 40-45 minutes in a 9x9 inch square pan. If you want larger but less thick brownies, bake in a 13x9 inch pan for 30 minutes.

Remove pan from oven. Wait 5 minutes then evenly sprinkle kosher salt on top of brownies. You don't want to heavily salt them, just a few coarse grains per brownie is fine. Let brownies cool then cut and remove from pan.

Yields 64 "brownie bites" or 35 larger flatter, brownies. Enjoy...

Yields 16 large brownies in a 9x9 pan that can then be cut into 64 bite- sized but thick pieces.

CHAPTER FIVE

What's in Your Fridge?

Much like our mothers and grandmothers who taught us to always have a nice pair of underpants on because you never know when you're going to get hit by a car and be taken in an ambulance to the hospital and strangers will see your underpants, I pay close attention to what's in my fridge and kitchen cupboards. Will I be embarrassed if guests come over and see that the entire top shelf of my fridge is filled with different kinds of cookies save one small box of whole grain Wasa? Not at all. I've got what I like to think is a healthy mix of a variety of foods that I love. Some are more healthful than others, it's true, but I have no shame in my package of Late July dark chocolate sandwich cookies. There's a time and a place.

Our kitchen pantries and refrigerators speak volumes about who we are; what we like to snack on, how prepared we are in terms of meal planning, how often we cook and how often we order in or go out. Are we freaks for salt or for sugar? Both? Is there a slice of cold pizza that will do nicely for breakfast or are you someone who has cereal, toast, juice and coffee every morning, just like the families in the 1970s TV commercials I used to watch? Who are you?

I talked to friends about their habits and what works for them. My friend Melissa tells me: "Recently I've tried to be better about buying and getting ready lots of fruits and vegetables, I also have carbs on hand that don't trigger me, like plain small sized whole wheat pitas. I'm only going to have one because they're not like chips for me, where I want to keep eating them. It's terrible to admit, but I find staying away from favorite "bad" stuff is better than depending on myself to have a little bit."

I like to make sure I always have lots of greens (kale!) and fruit and unsweetened almond milk and baby carrots and nuts on hand. I never go without a box or two of Kashi or Nature's Path cereal in the house and you will always find olive oil, tuna packed in water, whole-wheat pasta and barley in my cupboards. I do stock up on my fun fats too. I can't live without unsalted whipped butter and all-natural peanut butter. My fridge always has a couple of types of cheese, plain non-fat Greek yogurt, sometimes also a little bit of a flavored yogurt and I like to keep easy to grab veggie snacks- celery sticks, baby carrots, romaine or iceberg lettuce, endive and cherry tomatoes. I try not to stock too many "fake" foods, meaning things that are not really food but food-like. I don't buy processed junk, like snack crackers, cheese doodles and pop tarts. If I'm going to enjoy some cookies, then either I bake them myself from scratch, so I know just what's in them, or I buy ones that seem the most natural and have the least amount of ingredients and moreover, those that have ingredients that I can recognize. When I want to enjoy some chips, I buy potato chips that are made of potatoes, oil and salt- I stay away from the Doritos and the Cheetos. Those are good examples of processed "foods" that barely resemble anything that comes from the ground. I have not taken a liking to the new baked versions of chips. I find they taste like paper. If I'm going to have some chips, I'd rather have a few of something that tastes really good rather than a bag of baked chips that taste like, well, nothing.

I often have a box of organic vegetable broth on hand, so at a moment's notice I can whip up a soup if I'm in the mood. I often have a loaf of Ezekiel low glycemic raisin bread or Mestemacher whole grain flat bread and I am never without nuts-usually almonds and or walnuts. Berries! Oh how I love berries.

Depending on the season, you'll find blueberries, raspberries and strawberries in my fridge. I enjoy them with my cereal for breakfast and as snacks throughout the day, and as I've mentioned, I love taking a small bowl of berries and topping it with a spoon of ice cream.

In my freezer, there is very little. I tend to like things fresh. If I buy chicken, steaks or fish, I cook that within a day or two; I won't freeze it. Once in a while I'll freeze some sauce that I've cooked or a large batch of hearty soup or a lasagna. I always have a pint of Haagen Dazs ice cream on hand in the freezer and sometimes I will keep bags of frozen string beans, brussel sprouts, spinach or broccoli so I can just throw a couple of handfuls into a recipe when I want something green and don't feel like making a salad or cooking some kale. On occasion, I will stock up on some Amy's frozen cheese enchilada with black beans and corn entrees. That is about as processed as I get. The ingredients are pretty natural and Amy uses lots of organic foods in her meals. They taste fantastic.

You will not find any soda in my fridge unless I have guests who want it, but on rare occasions, I will have some diet caffeine free coke in there. There is always a pitcher of filtered water, but I don't buy juices or sugared drinks of any kind. When I think that someone drinking a regular 12 oz can of soda is getting the equivalent of 13 teaspoons of sugar, it makes me gasp. In the summer, I will often have a pitcher of plain cold tea on hand. I think one area in which I save a LOT of calories is my beverage consumption. I rarely drink coffee, but when I do I have it with cream and sugar, so clearly that would be an addition to my calorie intake. I drink plain tea and water and I never drink glasses of milk, I just use almond milk for my cereal in small amounts.

Also, I should mention that while I have a bottle of two of wine, whiskey, gin and the fixings for martinis and manhattans in my cupboards, I do drink very little alcohol. I know, 2/3 of you are now throwing the book down in disgust-well that's it! I'm doomed. I'm not saying that because I don't care that much for alcohol others shouldn't enjoy it, but I will suggest that certain types of alcoholic beverages, mixed drinks that have sugar and tasty flavorings especially, add a lot of calories to your diet and should not go unnoticed if you're trying to practice moderate consumption. For the more common plain alcoholic drinks, a 12 oz beer has 150 calories, a 4 oz glass of dry wine has 100 calories and a 1oz shot of 100 proof gin, vodka or whiskey has about 60 calories.

I've taken lately to buying organic brown eggs. I'm not a huge egg lover, but I like to have them on hand for the occasional omelet and for my baking. They cost more but I use them infrequently and I find they look so much healthier than eggs that come from hens that are not fed careful diets. When you crack the egg open, you can see how the organic egg's yolk stands up and doesn't mush out until you whip it up. It looks more robust and healthy. The regular egg's yolk flattens out immediately after coming out of the shell and the color is often not as bright. I feel better eating them-it might be psychological. My mission is not to engage in a debate about organic vs. non-organic foods, but rather to share with you why I choose what I do.

I want to talk about the plain yogurt in my fridge. I wasn't always a yogurt devotee. I used to hate yogurt, then I started enjoying coffee yogurt, but it was the only one I could stomach. The other flavors were too sweet for me. Once I started paying close attention to what I was putting in my body, I thought, *man, 25-30 grams of sugar for each 6 oz serving is a lot of sugar to be eating for one small coffee yogurt. Do I really need to eat that much sugar to enjoy it?* So I began trying plain yogurts. They were tough for me take at first but now, yogurt is one of my favorite foods. I think it's perfect, especially the strained Greek, non-fat ones. High in protein, low in carbs, plenty of calcium and if you eat the plain kind, low sugar content with no added sugars, only those occurring naturally in the milk. The hard part is adjusting to the plain. It's tart and can be a bit much for me sometimes. Here's my suggestion:

Take one small spoon of a flavored yogurt you like and add it to a 6 oz serving of plain non-fat yogurt. It will give it a little flavor so it's not quite so tart, and you'll enjoy a less sweet version of say, coffee yogurt, then you would normally have if you bought one of the yogurts that are loaded with sugar. Note-even the non-fat yogurts that are flavored have tons of sugar added and thus can make you fat, so do not be fooled by packaging that says "non-fat". The added sugar can certainly add on the pounds. If I add just a spoon of some flavor, I can make my serving of yogurt more enjoyable and not add many carbs or sugars. Sometimes, though, just adding a few strawberries sliced up or a handful of fresh blueberries can do the trick. Once, I even mixed in a little all natural peanut butter. Gross? You try it and then you judge me. You can also add a little crumbled Kashi or a cereal that's not too sugary that can give it a little crunch if that floats your boat. Just a little goes a long way. Remember, the idea is not to make everything about the fruit or nuts or crumbled cereal you're adding, but to keep it as low carb, low sugar of a snack as you can. If you load it up with chocolate chips and heaven forbid, gads of granola (although Kind now makes a granola that isn't too fattening and is less sugared up and I sometimes add ¼ cup to my plain yogurt) and Reese's peanut butter cups then you're missing the point. Keep it simple and you will enjoy the natural flavors.

So, to review, stock your fridge with healthy options and you will have less of a chance of snacking on junk food in the middle of the night! Give yourself every chance to succeed in having a well-planned healthy diet and start incorporating the foods you love into your healthy eating mindset.

Chocolate Chip Cookies

Inspired by Bobby Flay, tampered with by Karen

This is really a perfect chocolate chip cookie-I like to use whole wheat flour instead of white flour and all dark chocolate instead of half semi and half dark.

2 c and 3 tbsp flour

¾ tsp Kosher salt

¾ tsp baking soda

2 sticks butter, unsalted at room temp

2 large eggs

1 c granulated sugar

1/3 c dark brown muscovado sugar (don't substitute this really makes the flavor unbelievably rich)

1/3 c light brown muscovado sugar

10 oz dark chocolate chips (I like 60 % cacao or darker)

1 ½ tsp pure vanilla extract

Line baking sheet with parchment paper. Whisk together flour, salt, and baking soda and put in separate bowl. Beat butter 1 min with electric mixer until smooth. Add sugars and continue mixing, scraping sides of bowl and bottom til light and fluffy. Add eggs one at a time and then vanilla. Add half of flour mixture, then fold in remaining until just combined. Add chocolate chips.

Bake at 375 degrees 11 min. and rest for two min before removing cookies from sheet. Cool on rack.

Enjoy!

CHAPTER SIX

Slow and Steady Wins the Race

Slow down! It's not a race. Really, it's not. Unless, of course it IS a race and your name is either Joey Chestnut or Takeru Kobayashi and you're competing on July 4th in the annual hot dog eating contest. Then, it's a race. For the most part, there's rarely any occasion for you to be shoving food down your gullet without chewing it first.

I know; I do it too. It is partly the fault of the ridiculous, fast-paced lifestyles we lead. Eat on the go. I never sit down for breakfast when I have to go to work. Sound familiar? We want to sleep as late as we can in the morning, so we cram all of our morning duties into the smallest space humanly possible. I am usually much more concerned about which shoes I'm going to wear than I am about what I'm going to eat. Although, it's kind of funny because when I wake up I usually am happy that I can start another day of eating and I do give some thought to that. A clean slate. Haven't had any chocolate ALL DAY...

Here's the thing though: whether it's breakfast, lunch, dinner or a snack, eating slowly is one of the smartest eating habits you can have. Eating and chewing slowly allows you to pay closer attention to what you're eating, how much and how you feel as you're eating. Sometimes, I am in the middle of eating a meal and I realize- gosh, I'm full. Why make myself uncomfortable eating what some restaurant thinks is a serving of food? If I'm worried about appearing ungrateful at a host's house, then I apologize for having taken too much (if in fact it was self-serve, if not, then shame on them for piling it on my plate!). Once I realize that I'm sated then I should listen to my body, for it knows what it needs. Period. That old line my father used to tell me about how burping after a meal was a compliment to the chef is kind of gross. And unladylike. If you eat slowly, chewing thoroughly (everything I read says 20 chews per bite is a good number to shoot for) and taking the time to appreciate the meal you are having, you will be much more able to recognize the signs your body gives you when you've had enough. Especially if you know there's a delectable dessert coming down the pike-don't you want to also have room for a taste of whatever that's about? It's so nice to finish my meal, breathe, take some time to relax and then, maybe 20 minutes later, have a little something desserty.

All this talk of eating has gotten me hungry again for a snack. I've had breakfast already, about two hours ago, so I'm going to have one slice of this amazing natural dark brown whole grain pumpernickel bread that is very moist. Mestemacher is the brand. I am putting a small layer of whipped unsalted butter on it-less than 1/8 of an inch thick. Not a two-inch thick spread of butter. Hits the spot. The bread is so fibrous and hearty and flavorful. Totally kicks Wonder bread's ass. I top it with three thinly sliced pieces of beefsteak tomato and a pinch of kosher salt. I'm eating this snack way too quickly for someone who's writing this chapter, but it happens. I'm human.

Ok, so let's talk slow eating. What happens when you gobble that meatball hero in 4 minutes and maybe wash it down simultaneously with a soda? Well for starters, you've probably got indigestion. But even if you have an iron gut, you may not have needed to eat the whole hero right in that one 4 minute sitting. But you've already eaten it and in a few minutes you feel full and uncomfortable. Fun. When I listen to my body, when I sense the fullness even after half of what I intended to eat, then I know that's my body telling me: " Look, this is enough. Save it; we'll eat it later, but for now, really, I'm good." Your stomach is going to start to bulge out and that nosy lady on the 3rd floor is going to ask you if you're pregnant. The body is designed beautifully to process what we eat, if we don't abuse it. What constitutes abuse you ask? Just about everything most of us do during a meal.

I asked some of my friends how long they take to eat their meals, to see where I fit in. The average seems to be 10 minutes for lunch and 20-30 minutes for dinner. A good friend stated that she doesn't have a definitive lunch but rather eats periodically throughout the day, grazing at whatever she can find when she is hungry. Her busy work atmosphere does not allow for her to stop and sit down and have a meal. She goes on to say that she doesn't binge but she believes she overeats. At night, she often eats over the course of the evening and takes her time. She enjoys brunch on the weekends, when she has more time, and says she can often take a full hour to enjoy her meal. I've eaten with her and know that is true! She eats very slowly and is the kind of person who seems to naturally enjoy the experience of eating; the process, the conversation, and the atmosphere. She is less likely to overeat on those occasions when she has the time to sit and enjoy a specific meal, rather than when she is forced to grab nearby things that may not necessarily be the healthiest choices.

My first suggestion with lunch and dinner is to give yourself no less than 20 minutes to eat. Now, having worked in a fast-paced environment myself, I know that we don't always have the luxury of eating a meal in a quiet place where we aren't taking phone calls and getting asked to do this, that and the other thing. You can, however, take more control of your eating just by paying attention to your obstacles and making the best decisions you can.

Here's an example: in the morning, I leave myself about an hour to shower, get dressed, fix my hair and have breakfast before heading off to work. I never sit at any point during this routine; I just don't leave myself that kind of time. I need to multitask. I always have breakfast in the morning-usually Kashi cereal with almond milk and some blueberries or raspberries. I can either shovel it into my mouth in 3 minutes, which really would only serve to give me a stomach ache, or, as I have more recently learned, I can still eat my breakfast slowly if I take it with me, either into the bedroom or yes, sometimes the bathroom, but don't judge me please, I'm multitasking. If no one is using the toilet or the shower then it's just a room like any other room, isn't it? It's not like I have the cereal bowl in the toilet. I take a few bites and chew slowly while I am putting on make up, then I put the spoon down and do other things and then a few minutes later I have some more. I'm eating slowly while still meeting the needs of my morning routine. Conversely, if I feel the pressure of the time constraints and choose to wolf down my cereal in a few minutes, I feel stuffed, instead of nourished and ready to start my day.

Some mornings I feel like yogurt or some wholegrain toast. Because both of those foods can make me feel full very easily if I eat them too quickly, I might split the amount in two and take the second half with me for a second breakfast in a couple of hours. If I have a slice of toast with something already spread on it, I just fold it in half (to avoid a mess) and put it in a recyclable container and go. Or, if it's yogurt, I reseal it if possible and, if not, again, I place it in an airtight container in order to transport it. There is never a need to eat more than I need in the moment.

At the office, I often bring my lunch to my desk so I can multitask and return phone calls or do computer work while I eat. This potentially sets me up for more problems with rushed eating. I try to look at my computer clock and note the time I began my lunch so I can attempt to make the meal last at least 20 minutes. Also, I continually check to make sure I am chewing my food slowly. If something comes up and you have to quickly dash off to a last-minute meeting, don't wolf down what's left of your lunch just to finish. Rather, cover it, or put in the office fridge if necessary and possible, to be finished later, when you have the time to languish over it. I don't know why for years I felt forced to finish everything right there on the spot, as if someone was going to steal it from me if I didn't.

When I was in high school, I remember that the varsity club sold candy in the three minutes between class bells. This was done in the room where I had geometry class when I was fifteen. My class was at ten a.m. but that would often not deter me from getting some M&Ms. I was often bored out of my mind and I recall that I would try to make the package of candy last throughout the forty minute period. This did require some math on my part, although not geometry. I would count the M&Ms in the packet and then figure how many I could have in five-minute incremental periods to make them last the full class. It was something to do, and again, I say don't judge me because I had an A average in the class. I savored each candy-coated, colored chocolate piece because I knew I had to make them last. If I could do that with a packet of M&Ms, I am sure that we can make an entire meal last for twenty minutes.

If you live with others, it might be easier to make your meals stretch out over a longer period of time when you are at home. When you have several people living with you and you eat meals together, you are probably more apt to take your time and have discussions while you eat, slowing you down (in theory). Even if it's only you and a partner or a roommate, use that to your advantage and try and sit down and have your meals at the table, facing each other, enjoying conversation and taking your time with your meal.

If you live alone, fear not. There are things you can do to slow yourself down:

1) If you must have dessert-choose to wait to have it later and let yourself digest your meal a bit. You may even find that you don't have room for as much of a dessert as you initially expected. And if you've got something really great for dessert, how nice would it be to have it tomorrow evening as well, if you ate only half tonight?

2) Do you have a fun 30-minute show that you have recorded with your DVR and are waiting to see?   If you play it back fast-forwarding through the commercials, it should run about 22 minutes. If you can make your dinner last for the whole show; you'll be doing fine! And you will have caught up on a show without wasting time since it was mealtime anyway.

3) Treat yourself to a little elegance. Instead of taking your plate on your lap with a paper towel, put out a tablecloth or placemat, use your nice dishes, cloth napkins, maybe even pour yourself a glass of wine. Just going through the motions of having a fancier meal makes me slow down. Having a cloth napkin forces me to delicately dab it around my mouth in between bites. You can still have a sit-down meal if you're eating alone. No need to scarf everything down because no one is watching. It actually feels kind of nice to take the time to treat yourself well at mealtime.

When I eat alone, I do find it challenging to fight the urge to eat quickly and to pay attention to what I'm eating. Sure, one of the advantages of eating alone is that you are free to do whatever you want for your meal. If you want to have cereal for dinner, you can. But that doesn't mean you have to eat like a pig. When you have the time, plan a balanced meal, prepare it with love (for both yourself and the delicious food) and then sit down and slowly enjoy every morsel. Mark the end of a trying day with a relaxing meal.

Even if you are having a pb&j sandwich with some celery sticks, this too can be savored. Cut the sandwich into quarters; decorate the plate with the placement of the vegetables. Go crazy and throw some parsley onto the plate! Pretend you've ordered the sandwich and it's being served to you. Make it fun. Make the meal about more than just shoveling food into your mouth. Make it artful and pleasing to the eye as well as to the palate. Anything you can do to force yourself to think about what you're eating and slow the heck down, will be well worth it.

KAREN'S SNACK BOX

Whole grain pumpernickel bread

-one slice

1 tbsp whipped unsalted butter

3 thinly sliced tomato slices

a pinch of kosher salt

CHAPTER SEVEN

Dining Out

I live in New York City. There are heaps of wonderful restaurants. People love to eat out-I get it. It's fun, it's often sociable, it's tasty, and it's convenient. But... it can make eating within your caloric means difficult. While it's true that more and more eating establishments are offering nutritional information, restaurants are in the business of selling food. That means they add as much as they can get away with to make things taste amazing. Often after eating a delectable piece of beautifully cooked salmon at a restaurant, I'll say to myself, I could make a piece of fish taste that good too if I cooked it in a stick of butter.

What to do, what to do? This is my strongest event in the eating games. I can eat out, be it in a hospital cafeteria, or a fancy Manhattan restaurant and I won't let all hell break loose and yet I'll still enjoy myself immensely. I'll give you some scenarios-play along...

I'm at my favorite Brooklyn diner having a chicken salad sandwich. Who knows how much mayo they put in their salad? I don't. I do notice they pack on the chicken salad though; the sandwich is about three or four inches thick. I still want to enjoy the chicken salad and yet I don't want to over eat or fill up on too much bread. I love the taste of the chicken salad on whole wheat toast, though. What's a girl to do? I take the chicken salad off of the bread and put half of it aside. I will ask for a disposable container and take half of the salad home and have it for another meal. I then put 3 of the 4 pieces of bread to the side. I don't need to eat all of that bread. I simply take one of the quarters of the toast and eat that with the chicken salad. I get to enjoy the taste of the crisp toast with the chicken salad and yet I'm eating only ¼ of the amount of bread they served me. It tastes the same, just less bread and less filling. The idea is to eat MORE of the protein, the chicken, and less of the carb, the bread, not the other way around.

I attend a weekly work meeting on Fridays where they serve lunch. Lunch consists of a green salad, an assortment of sandwich halves and bags of baked potato chips. There are also cans of soda available, diet and regular and a pitcher of ice water flavored with some citrus fruit. What do I have? Well, for starters, I take plenty of salad (I hope you're starting to see a theme here...), no chips – frankly, if they were real Lays, I'd have some. I take a sandwich half or two, but because the sandwiches are really mostly thick pieces of the whitest bread possible, I take the meat or cheese and any veggies out and mix it in with my salad. I look at the bread as if it's a donut or a big piece of cake, because, although it may not have much fat itself, it's used for its sugar in the body which is digested quickly while the fat stays in my body, unused. If I want a piece of the tasty sourdough yumminess then I have a bite or two, but I almost always leave the bread portions behind. I then lightly dress the salad with an olive oil vinaigrette or I eat it plain. And I usually drink the water although every so often I'm up for a Diet Coke. I don't particularly like the sweetness of a sugary soda, nor do I want the 13 teaspoons of sugar that come with it.

Now I can sit there in that meeting and have the same lunch offered to me as someone else, but if my colleague is having little or no salad, two sodas, and two or three sandwich halves with all of the bread and a bag or two of chips (because they are BAKED after all so they must be healthy so why not have two?) think of how many more carbs and sugars he is consuming. There we were, having ostensibly, the same lunch, with a few key changes. I was eating a low calorie, high fiber nutrient dense lunch, whereas he was having mostly sugar. I find it very interesting. People might assume they are serving a healthy lunch-turkey sandwich, salad, baked chips not fried, but if it's consumed in a certain manner, it can be a meal which prevents you from keeping pounds off.

I noticed that at a different conference I attended, I was seated at a table with several other people from my workplace whom I did not know, and one of my everyday co-workers whom I know quite well. Three of the ladies were at least 20 lbs overweight. There were three of us who were at a healthy weight for our respective sizes. At the lunch break, they served us–what else... a buffet of various sandwiches, tossed green salad, baked chips, soft drinks, water and assorted cookies and brownies. I could not help but notice that my co worker and I took mostly salad and then one half of a sandwich which we both dismantled to reveal the vegetables and protein from the inside of the bread. We both left the white roll behind on our plates. Neither of us took the chips. We both drank water. I had a small, bite-sized brownie and she had none of the sweets. The colleagues on the other side of the table ate the bread, the chips, the sugared soft drinks and not only ate the large cookies offered but at one point, one of the women brought back a plate of cookies " for the table" and set them down in the middle. I ate none. My coworker ate none. The cookie-bearer proceeded to eat three of the large cookies.   I'm talking four inches in diameter. And she was quite overweight.

People who don't think about what they are putting in their mouths, and don't make conscious choices to be healthy, end up being overweight. That doesn't have to be you. Even if that's who you were, you don't have to be that person any longer. I didn't always make smart food choices. I learned. I learned what works for me, what satisfies me, what I love to eat, what I can live without, what I absolutely cannot live without. It's not magic. It's common sense.

College can be the toughest years. For some who live in dorms, as I did, it's four years of eating out, in a sense. One doesn't get to decide what dishes will be served in a dining hall. And during those four years our bodies are often still changing and declaring themselves. It's a recipe for disaster. I alluded earlier to the famed Freshman Fifteen. I was in that club, my friends.

Ah, college dining halls. Ours was called the All Campus Dining Center, or ACDC. I initially thought it was a nice tribute to the rock band from the 1970s/80s. After having been the meal preparer for the previous nine years at home, along with my sister, it was a nice break to consider just walking into this large, rather pleasant brick building and having all of my meals already made for me. And no dishes to do! And because I had the three meals a day, seven days a week meal plan, it deceptively seemed that everything was free. I could gather with my friends, sit and eat, go back for seconds, thirds if I wanted. What was not to love about ACDC?

When you're 18-22 years old, chances are you are not thinking so much about watching your weight, your caloric intake, your fats, your carbs, and your sugars. Heck, back when I was that age, no one talked about watching carbs. Carbs were considered to be the good thing that you were *supposed to eat*, especially those that did not have a lot of fat. Load up on the cereal, cereal is healthy! Yes the kinds I enjoyed were coated in layers of sugar but how can cereal be bad for you? It's a grain.

If I could go back and do college again and have another crack at ACDC, here's what I'd do: 1) I'd limit myself to ONE 8 oz. bowl of cereal in the morning and I'd make sure that ¾ of it was a non-sugary whole grain like shredded wheat. 2) I'd allow myself to mix in a small amount of the sugary cereal like Lucky Charms or Cocoa Puffs, just for a little flavor. Two ounces is not a lot. 3) I'd have a half cup of some berries or banana in the morning with my cereal, to give myself some natural sweetness and some added fiber and vitamins. 4) I'd eat some protein with that meal instead of more carbs like a bagel or toast. I'd have some nuts or some peanut butter or perhaps an egg or some plain yogurt.

Lunch at ACDC was also dangerous territory-tuna tetrazzini was my favorite. The starchier, the better. Give me something sticky and white with visible starch on it and I was in heaven, especially on a cold wintry day in Poughkeepsie. The odds are often stacked against us when we walk into any eating establishment. Unless you are preparing your own meals at home, you can't be sure what you're eating and how they are making the food so appetizing. That means we have to be hypervigilant when dining out, even at the finest of restaurants. Not that you can't enjoy a meal at a five star restaurant, but here are some tips:

1) Drinks. When the waiter asks for a drink order, start with water, then consider what you'll be eating and pick something you'd like to enjoy with your meal. I suggest one glass of wine and no more than two. Drink in moderation. Just because it's not solid does not mean it can't pack on the pounds. Alcohol has calories and mixed drinks with sugary additives can be particularly caloric. Would you like a nice shot of Bailey's Irish Cream in your coffee? There's 94 calories in a 1.3 oz shot. I'm not saying not to have it ever, but if you do have it, maybe you should consider skipping dessert.

2) Bread. Mmm. Warm, freshly baked bread is enticing. It's not an appetizer. Don't eat the whole basket. Take one or two small slices and put it on your bread plate. Take a bite or two when it arrives and then save the rest for

your meal. Close the napkin over the basket to prevent yourself from staring at it.

3) Appetizers. If you're dining out with others and want to share some different appetizers, make sure not to over order. You can always order more if you must, but chances are you will be satisfied having a taste of a couple of different things. Remember, it's not the meal, it's not supposed to fill you up, it's supposed to whet your appetite for the entrée.

4) Sauces and dressings. Many restaurants use delicious, creamy, fatty, highly caloric sauces to serve over their main course and this can often include the vegetables. They are good. No reason you can't savor the flavor of a tasty béchamel sauce, but do so in moderation. No need to eat every bit of sauce poured on the meat. I will often take a knife and scrape 80% of the sauce off of the meat so I can still appreciate the flavor. Watch salad dressings too-sometimes the veggies are doused in lots of dressing. A good restaurant usually doesn't

overdo it and there's just the right amount of flavor. When possible, I ask for dressings on the side so I have more control over what I use.

5) Dessert. I make a habit of splitting desserts with my fellow diners, especially at an expensive restaurant where they charge $14 for a piece of cake. Even if it's a tiny piece, as it often is in the fancy schmancy places, it still helps to know I'll just be taking a few bites. After a small taste of something rich, I usually feel satisfied.

Last week, I was out to breakfast at a typical American diner, like a Denny's, and I noticed that the menu included calories along with the picture of the decadent offerings. I was in the mood for French toast and saw that as pictured, it would have been 1140 calories. That is a good percentage of the calories someone my size can eat in a day. That was for three slices of French toast, bacon and ham, potatoes, butter and syrup. I was not deterred! I ordered the French toast, a la carte, and when I became full after two pieces with a modicum of syrup and a tiny bit of butter, I called it quits. No need to overindulge, no matter how tempting they try to make it! So, go out and eat and enjoy, but do it wisely.

Summer Chopped Vegetable Salad

2 medium beefsteak tomatoes

1 large cucumber (I like to remove the skin but not   necessary)

2 scallions

8 or 10 small champignon (button) white mushrooms

2 stalks celery

Olive oil and lemon juice, salt and pepper to taste

Chop all ingredients to your desired size (I like things pretty small) and place in large salad bowl. Add olive oil and lemon juice to your liking, along with a little salt and black pepper.

Enjoy this fresh, easy to make summer salad. It's a great way to enjoy lots of veggies.

CHAPTER EIGHT

Snacks

I never like to position myself so that the only things I have around me are highly caloric (unless I'm on a long hike) or junky foods without nutrients. I try to think ahead, so that when I do enjoy things like nuts and chocolate, I have a fairly good idea of how much of them I am eating. If someone hands me a bag of chocolate chips to snack on, I might eat much more than I intended to. If I pack my own snacks in portioned out sizes, however, then I can control how much I eat without fear of losing myself in the moment.

As I mentioned earlier, I try not to deprive myself of foods or snacks that I feel like having. I derive great pleasure from eating. I rarely tell myself I can't have something because I know enough to have just a small taste of something that's purely decadent and that provides little nutrition. My standard way of eating is actually snacking. I have more trouble with the three-square–meals-a-day model, as I feel uncomfortable after eating just a portion of one of those meals and have to stop. I end up separating most of those meals into twos and threes anyhow. I'm a born snacker. Let me show you how I roll...

Breakfast. As I've stated previously, I often eat a small bowl of cereal with berries and sometimes a little yogurt in the morning. If I have time, I brew a cup of hot red rooibos tea. I then get hungry in about two hours, so I have to make sure to have breakfast snacks with me at the office. I keep Greek yogurt on hand, as well as peanut butter, sometimes cut up veggies and fruit, always nuts and dark chocolate. I might bring a slice of Ezekiel sprouted grain bread with me. If I have a small breakfast at home at 7:30, come 9:30 or 10:00, I need something else. I might take 4 oz. of plain fat free Greek yogurt and cut up half of a large banana in it. Or I spread a tablespoonful of natural peanut butter on the bread. If I bring cookies to work for my morning or afternoon tea, I PORTION them out so that I'm not bringing a box or a bag and thinking it will last me a week or two. I take one or two small cookies and put them in a container and bring them each day. Trust me, it really helps to control the portions.

If you're someone who loves cereal but doesn't really feel hungry enough to eat before you leave the house, bring a small container (1 cup full) of your favorite NON-sugary cereal. If your workplace allows for it, bring some berries too and have your bowl of cereal at your desk with milk or yogurt. If not, bring the cereal and snack on it during the morning, but I do suggest you limit yourself to one portion and not snack out of the box or bag. This applies to packing snacks for your kids, too. If you put some cereal in a container for them, make sure it's not more than you intended it to be-½ cup is usually a serving, so try to limit it to two servings at the most. Kids can pack on the pounds too. You'll want to vary their snacks so not all of them come in the form of carbohydrates. Try packing part skim milk string cheese or carrots and celery sticks maybe with a small container of natural peanut or other nut butter for a "dip". A small box of raisins or other dried fruit in moderation also makes a good, high-energy snack. Try to avoid packing chips, crackers, cookies. If you make your own cookies and know what's in them and want to pack them one or two, fine. But make sure to pack other items, which are not high in added sugar and hopefully also with some protein, to provide some balance.

Some foods are packaged and marketed specifically as snack sizes or snack foods, often for children. I would avoid pudding snacks as they are loaded with added sugar and instead I'd look for natural applesauce or a plain non-fat yogurt or a lightly flavored one, maybe something you mix up yourself. Remember that pre-packaged items are often sold for the sake of convenience, not nutrition. If you pack a few slices of Wasa or a handful of whole grain crackers and an ounce of organic cheese instead of those pre-packaged Ritz-type snack crackers and processed-cheese-like-food cheeses, you're getting more nutrition and thus, your snack will pack more punch. The idea is to make the most out of the little snacks that we indulge in so they do get you and your kids to the next meal feeling satisfied.

Refrain from packing any kind of candy as a snack, either for you or your kids. Most of us get offered candy from time to time out in the world either at the office or at school or at a party. If we don't keep it in our homes, then we are less likely to eat it there, which is one step ahead of the game. If one keeps a bag of let's say... candy corn, in one's kitchen cabinet, it is a LOT more likely to wind up on someone's peanut butter sandwich then if it hadn't been in the cabinet in the first place. Ok, that someone is I. If I have candy corn in the house I most certainly WILL put it on my sandwich at some point. That's my ugly side. If it's not in the house, you won't fall prey to its devilish charms. If you are offered a lovely chocolate truffle or some Twizzlers or a Kit Kat or whatever does it for you and you're not always munching on that stuff at home, then you won't feel so bad having it when you do indulge and you can better enjoy it for the treat that it is. Furthermore, if you teach your children early on that candy is something to be enjoyed in moderation and is not a necessary part of every meal, you will be doing them a sweet favor.

I think one of the best snacks to pack is fruit (in moderation!). Berries, apple slices, bananas, oranges, plums and clementines are my favorites. They usually travel fairly well and aren't too messy to eat (although I've done battle with some uncooperative oranges). When I'm walking around the city and really need a snack and want to avoid grabbing a candy bar or a sugary granola bar, I will often grab a banana from a deli. Berries aren't exactly finger foods and can make for a messy snack, but sometimes I will bring along some large, ripe strawberries.

Let's do talk for a minute about granola bars. The category has become vast over the last decade. You can find nutrient-dense, less sugary bars and you can find some granola bars that are worse than some candy bars as far as added refined sugars are concerned. And then there are protein bars. Some of those also have a lot of added garbage in them. I try to find ones with the least amount of ingredients, made from identifiable items. So many bars have ingredient lists with compound words that just seem very unlike food and more like a chemical experiment or some kind of futuristic project. Sure, they are convenient, but how healthy can they be? And don't get me started on the ones with substitute sugars, they taste even less like real food to me and strangely sweet. I encourage you to read the labels and know exactly what you're putting into your kids' lunches or your own gym bag. My favorites lately are Pure bars and Kind bars. Just a few recognizable ingredients in each and they taste like food.

Please notice that "snack" is not a four–letter word. There's nothing wrong with snacking as long as it's done with thought and not as part of a constant shoveling of food into one's mouth. Snacking might be vitally important to your lifestyle and can many times be more cost-effective than eating large meals out. But it does have to be done with planning and common sense.

KAREN'S SNACK BOX

Trail Mix combo:

Combination of walnuts, dark chocolate pieces, or use Ghirardelli dark chocolate chips, almonds, dried cranberries, pumpkin seeds.

I wouldn't bring more than a handful's worth for a regular day snack, two or three times that if you're going to the gym or hiking and burning lots of extra calories.

It's a great hiking or pre-gym combo or if you're out shopping or doing errands and you get hungry-much better to grab a handful of my mix then a processed candy bar or cookies. It's got protein, omega 3s, fiber, healthy fats, and antioxidants. You can control the amount of sugar and carbs by going easy on the chocolate and cranberries.

CHAPTER NINE

The Chicken or the Egg?
How I Stay Fit with Regular Moderate Exercise

Every so often, someone comments on my commitment to exercise, or my practice of moderation in eating by telling me that I don't need to watch my diet or I don't need to exercise because I'm little. "You can eat whatever you want!" I think they have it backwards: I'm slim because I take care of my body, I watch what I eat and I exercise regularly. Not fanatically, but regularly. Don't get scared away. In order to remain slim, I need to continue to exercise. Nobody gets a free pass. A healthy, strong, fit body takes work. Accept that and we'll get along just fine. Seriously. If you think

I'm thin at age 47 because I'm lucky, you're wrong.

When you're seven years old and you can eat anything you want and you burn off all of the calories you consume in a day and you're making mud pies and chasing your friends around the block and riding your bike and jumping in the pool, ok, ok, then you can maybe say you're lucky, maybe. But is that kid really lucky or is he really just a very good example of balance at its best? Kids eat tons of calories but kids BURN tons of calories and of course they are growing at the speed of light so they have the metabolisms to support such an intake. I'm guessing that those of us reading this book are not growing at the speed of light, at least not upwards. My friend Joseph says he can point to one period in his life when he was able to achieve a desirable balance. Going to the gym regularly allowed him to eat whatever he wanted and not gain weight. Which was the whole point in working out for him. But other than those two or three years, he has never been able to find the right balance. Interesting, without the exercise the equation can't work.

I also interviewed David, who has come to appreciate the necessity of exercise and even learned to like it : "My metabolism and need to exercise has changed dramatically over the years. In my late teens and 20s, I could eat whatever I wanted and exercise very little and my weight was fine. That all changed as I approached 30, coupled with my quitting smoking at 32. At that point I realized that I had gained quite a bit of weight (about 30 pounds in ten years) and began to pay very close attention to my diet and workout regimen and I've gotten more and more strict since then. I am very happy with my current weight, though I'd probably be happier if I were about 5 pounds lighter. I have to work very hard to maintain the weight I'm at. I work out 5 times a week, for 45 minutes to an hour and I'm careful with my eating most days (not on vacation). I know exactly how much exercise I need to do and how much food I can eat and maintain my weight, but it's not even close to the amount I would like to eat, though I've learned to love exercise and even if I didn't need to, to maintain my weight and maintain good health, I still would choose to".

David recognizes that although he would love to eat more, he can't. He understands the relationship between how much he eats, how much he exercises and how much he weighs, and he balances himself. I like that David also told me he doesn't think about what he's eating so much on vacation-he just likes to enjoy himself, and knows that because exercise is a regular part of his life, he will again find that balance.

It's time for a snack that's on the sweet side. I'm going to have a Clementine (in the orange family but much smaller) and one slice of Ezekiel raisin bread with some thinly spread dark chocolate peanut butter. Note that I've used less than a tablespoon of peanut butter. With butter or peanut butter or olive oil, I always try to use the least amount possible to still give me flavor.

Ok, let's talk about exercise. I was never a particularly athletic child and I rarely played sports, except when forced by my gym teacher to chase after a soccer ball or stand in the outfield staring at the sun and praying the ball didn't get hit toward me. I wasn't particularly coordinated when it came to sports and if I was spared the embarrassment of always being picked last on a team, it was only because my endless enthusiasm and well-developed social skills landed me the title of "good for team morale" so I was usually next to the last picked:

"Well, at least she's got spunk. We'll take Wexler on our team."

I didn't have to walk to school like some kids-my siblings and I took the bus seven miles back and forth daily, so I didn't do a lot of walking. I always liked running around and the feeling of being winded after a sprint and having to catch my breath after I did something seemingly athletic. On field day, even though I only took home the green Participant badges and never placed in any race, I felt like an Olympic athletic and it felt good. I liked the feeling of having energy and using my muscles, small as they were, to take my body to new heights.

When I became a sophomore in high school, I decided to follow in my sister's footsteps and try out for cheerleading. I couldn't do a split or anything that resembled a decent cartwheel, but, thankfully, they needed someone pint-sized to throw on top of the pyramids, so I was in. For the first time in my life, I had a regular workout routine, each day after school at cheering practice. I learned to stretch my muscles before and after practice. I remember feeling so sore the first few days after practice began each semester, and how good that kind of sore felt. My first experience with "good sore".

There was usually a 45-minute period between the time school ended and the time cheering practice began. My fellow cheerleaders and I would often walk up to the Grand Union grocery store at the top of the hill about a fifth of a mile from the school. We'd often get a candy bar for a pre-cheering snack. My favorite combo was a York Peppermint Patty and a Diet Pepsi. If I could go back in time, I might change that to a flavored water or a plain ice tea and a handful of nuts with some pieces of chocolate. I can't imagine that my snack gave me that much energy.

As a high school student, I used to love to read not only teen magazines but those designed for adult women, too. Glamour, Mademoiselle and Cosmo come to mind. I was always trying the exercises they wrote about to help one get rid of weird sounding ailments like saddlebags and thunder thighs. To this day I still don't really know what a saddlebag looks like on the body but it sounds unpleasant. At fifteen, I started doing the exercises not because I felt, "wow I could use some toning up", but rather as a proactive measure. I wanted to be fit. I wanted to have the best body I could have, scrawny, chicken-legged little thing that I was, with acne, big poufy hair and a nose that had grown faster than the rest of my face. During those tumultuous teen years, my muscles seemed like the one thing over which I could exercise some control.

Mild exercise became a way of life for me. At the time, we used to call it calisthenics. I didn't have dumbbells in my basement, and I wasn't taking gymnastics nor was I on the softball team. I liked to run around and I liked feeling fit. That's basically how I feel today, in my forties. What happened in between those thirty years? I'm glad you asked...

College. Although I did succumb to the loathed Freshman Fifteen, I actually tried to stay somewhat active. There was quite a lot of walking around campus to get from building to building and to meals in the dining hall, and my friends and I would make dates to go to the fitness center on campus and use the Nautilus weight machines. I also availed myself of ballet classes and squash classes, both good workouts in very different ways. Then there were student taught classes available in the College Center. I remember signing up for Body Sculpting and needing to buy 2 lb weights and thinking they were so heavy to carry home from the store. We would listen to Spandau Ballet while we performed a series of light toning movements choreographed by our teacher, a fellow student who wanted to help us combat Freshman Fifteen.

At that time, as much as I felt I was being active, I had trouble keeping weight off. I liked to eat quite a lot back then and clearly I was eating more calories than I needed to, based on photographic evidence from the mid 1980s. There was a classmate of mine who I thought had the perfect figure. She had years of dancing training and a willowy, lithe frame that I envied. She was, what I considered to be the perfect height, probably 5'5" and had long blonde wavy hair. When I stood beside her, I felt like a gumdrop standing next to a Twizzler.

I decided to observe her behavior. I had breakfast with her and would see that she was having granola and yogurt and she was eating it slowly. In those days, eating granola was considered a very healthy thing to do. Not that it's particularly unhealthy now, but we have found ways to make it less so. The conversation she was involved in always seemed more important to her than what she was eating. She was one of those people that seemed capable of going on indefinitely without thinking about her next meal. It made me hate her a little bit. Eating was an afterthought for someone like her, not a raison d'etre.

Most important, what I noticed about her was that she was very physical, very active. She was always taking dance classes, exercising, stretching, moving her body. She was on to something-move more, eat less. Four years of college and at least I took that principle with me.

After I graduated and moved to New York City, I soon became part of a wonderful walking culture. Walking EVERYWHERE. For the first time in my life, I would sometimes walk miles a day. Because I was a poor, "starving", actress when I arrived on Manhattan's Upper East Side, I took a sublet which was cheap and thus very far from the closest subway. It was a good 15-20 minute walk to the closest train, and with the added 30-40 minutes of brisk walking a day (I tend to be a fast walker, not a stroller) I began to notice my body getting leaner. I should give some credit to the obvious fact that I was no longer on the generous college meal plan, getting all the food I wanted, that I was now paying for my meals, budgeting for groceries and eating modestly. On a waitress's tips, one had to spend carefully. And this did not include all of the walking I did going to auditions, getting from here to there addition and walking to and from the subway to go home. The city had become my glitzy and glamorous cardio machine!

A few years later, I changed living scenarios and took a studio apartment on the Upper West Side. There, although I was only two blocks from the subway, I was in a five-flight walk up building on the top floor. This meant sixty-some odd steps up and down each time I wanted to leave my apartment, with no option of an elevator. My own Stairmaster! No membership to a gym required. And each time I schlepped groceries up those stairs, I got an extra boost of a workout. For the first time in my life, I actually had a behind. A real round behind. Not that scrawny excuse of a backside that I had come to know and not love, a real ass!

It was also at this time that I began taking jazz classes twice a week at a nearby dance studio. The teacher was tough as nails and had made us all fear that if we didn't learn to use our glutes, they would soon enough start to slide down the back of our legs. I imagined that was right up there with saddlebags, and opted not to wait for that horrid fate. Having had no formal dance training other than the semesters of ballet that I took in college, I was having the time of my life dancing and working out at a barre.

The class was made up of non-dancers, professional dancers who just wanted a "kick your ass" kind of workout to stay in shape in between shows, and people like me, or as my teacher called us, "the moves wells". We were people who could move around quite gracefully

156

and learn a routine but you wouldn't see us dancing for our dinner on stage. Because of the varied talent levels and experience in the class, the dance routines at the end of the workout part of the class were not complicated and intended to make us move and have fun and enjoy the music. To this day, 20 years later, I still do the Anita Baker "Rapture" routine and the Jennifer Holliday " And I am Telling You I'm not Going" routine from Dreamgirls. As nutty as that teacher could be, that class made me enjoy getting exercise in a way that also fed my soul.

The pattern I want you to see here, is that I've found ways to evolve with my changing surroundings and utilize both free sources of exercise in my environment and local options, that didn't take much effort on my part to get there.

Before I continue, I need some lunch. There's a chill in the air and I am in the mood for something warm and hearty. I am going to heat up some of the soup I made this past weekend. I like making a big batch of something healthy and then freezing part of it and keeping part of it on hand in the fridge. I find if I have something healthy available, I'm more likely to make wise choices than if I just scour the cupboards looking for something to jump out at me. That's when I run the risk of making a peanut butter and candy corn sandwich... This soup is great and I've tailored it to my preferences. It's a recipe from Mario Batali for vegetable faro soup with pinto beans. I don't love pinto beans, and can never find faro, so I make it with barley and small white beans and leave the vegetables the same (although sometimes I add some kale at the end for extra fiber and vitamins). It's easy to make, very tasty, and vegetarian, for when I feel like a meatless meal. I sometimes take one thin slice of pumpernickel or spelt bread and put on a couple teaspoons of all natural peanut butter and enjoy it with the soup.

Back to exercise! Around the same time I was enjoying the jazz class, I discovered that a 10-minute walk from my apartment landed me at the Central Park reservoir. Home to many wonderful scenes from movies and television shows set in New York City, the reservoir is a beautiful place to have a walk, a run, or just people watch. The latter, however, probably doesn't burn many calories.

A couple of quick-paced laps around the reservoir provided me a nice chunk of cardio exercise. I'd often bring my Walkman (yes it was that long ago) and listen to wonderful cassette tapes made especially for me by my dear friend, Joseph. Sometimes I'd have Yankee games on the radio to keep me company as I did my laps. Once in a while, I'd let my mind wander and I'd fantasize that I'd meet JFK, Jr. on one of my laps, and he would of course fall madly in love with me at first glance. He was often photographed jogging in the park, so why not? It could happen.

During the years before I forked over the money to join a gym, I would mix my cardio workouts with my own combination of free weight exercises that I had gleaned from years of taking various classes and watching exercise shows. Sometimes I would add a little ballet barre workout that felt right, or some of the other exercises from that crazy jazz class that worked for me. The point is, I never stopped exercising and I never did it fanatically, either. There was always a nice balance of weight training and cardio that I looked to as a way of life, and my routines have evolved with my body's needs and my changing tastes.

In the winter of 2000, perhaps as part of a subconscious new millennium resolution, I decided to take the plunge and shell out the 75 bucks a month to join the local gym. It actually wasn't a bad price for a gym in Manhattan, and I received a discount through my workplace to join this particular chain. My gym was one block from my apartment, but I had to pass Zabar's to get there, and my downfall has always been their chocolate croissants. They were so very buttery and easy to eat-they melted in my mouth. Filled with chocolate-not just at the ends so it seemed as though you're getting a filled croissant, it was really, really packed with chocolate. And at Zabar's, the croissants were often warm, fresh out of the oven. If ever there was an impetus to get one's ass to the gym...

I digress. At my gym, I got into the habit of doing 20-30 minutes of cardio and a 20

 minute weight workout two or three times a week. Twelve years later, I still have the same practice- I go to the gym two or three times a week TOPS, and I don't work out more than 45-50 minutes; I just can't bear to stay longer than that. Once I've exercised, I always feel so happy to have done it and it feels good both physically and mentally, but like most people, I wish I could be fit and toned without having to do the work. I do think that making it something I do regularly helps keep me on track. My good friend, Catherine, points out how exercise and eating well go hand in hand for her:

"If I reach a period of high stress and an overly busy schedule, my exercising falls off, while at the same time I am eating more because of stress, and then I gain weight. And once you break the exercise habit, it is hard to get back into it."

Also in 2000, I began studying yoga. First, I took classes offered for staff at my workplace, and then I would drop by classes at my gym and learned varying styles of yoga-vinyasa, hatha, kundalini. Some poses reminded me of many exercises from the past and felt comfortable, some challenged me in new ways, and some proved too much for the limitations of my body and my mind. I found the whole process of learning about yoga interesting, and decided I wanted it to remain in my life, even if I couldn't always attend classes. Because of my battle with acid reflux, I found that many positions exacerbated the reflux so I felt like a pain in the tush, always telling the instructors at the beginning of the class what my issues were so that they could modify the poses for me. I could never do anything inverted-including downward dog(a staple in many yoga classes), nor could I do any backbends or shoulder, head or handstands. Ok, fair enough, I couldn't do a handstand anyway. Ever. Even when I was 8.

I started doing yoga at home, incorporating it into my life almost daily-with a fifteen or twenty-minute yoga practice here and there. I sometimes do yoga watching one of my favorite Sunday morning shows-the Sports Reporters. It helps me start off my Sunday with a relaxed, open and flexible body. Ideally, one is supposed to practice yoga either in silence or with appropriate music to enhance the poses and the breathing, television is antithetical to the practice, but hey, whatever works for you, works for you. I'm neither a purist nor a snob when it comes to exercise of any kind. Sometimes, I find upon waking that a 10-minute yoga routine involving sun salutations, tree and eagle poses is enough to help me comfortably begin my day.

Over the last ten years or so, I have gotten into a bit of a regular routine with working out that really seems to fit my needs. While I haven't strayed too much from the cardio, weights and yoga mix, I have tried to keep myself open to different forms of each, and I mix it up when I can, to keep some variety and save me from utter boredom. For instance, as a city dweller, I am thrilled at the chance to have a nice hike in the country with fresh air, when the opportunity arises. I enjoy hiking and can walk for hours as long as I have enough water and am wearing the proper footwear. Also, I would gladly substitute a nice walk outside at a brisk pace in the city, for a 30-minute session on a treadmill. Anytime I am able to walk anywhere, I do, and the longer the better. Those of us who don't own cars, often rely on our physical strength to schlep groceries, shelving from Bed Bath and Beyond, sometimes furniture. We burn calories all day long in many ways. When I used to live in that five-flight walk-up I would have the added calorie buster of the 68 steps, often a few times a day. Now with an elevator building, I sometimes take the stairs just for fun!

Exercise has always been an integral part of my healthy lifestyle, but eating to fit the amount of physical activity I do on a given day is also important. On days when I'm home most or all of the day, I eat less. I do it instinctively. My body doesn't need as much to stay fulfilled as on days when I'm prancing all over town or doing heavy exercise such as hiking. I don't deprive myself of foods I love on those quieter days; I just eat a little less of them.

I've often heard people say they can eat anything in sight while they are on vacation and don't seem to gain weight. My friend Nancy and I marveled that she actually had a concave belly while we traveled together in Italy, land of pasta and gelato. When I've been traveling (note I said traveling, not necessarily vacationing and lying on a beach, sedentary), I notice that I seem to be able to eat and eat and eat and I don't gain weight. I must be burning so many calories running through airports and carrying luggage and then walking all over a new town that I require more food. Give the body what it needs, and stop when it's had enough.

On days when I'm home sick with a cold or the flu, I eat applesauce, toast, tea, maybe some soup. I don't drop more than a pound though, even though I'm consuming very little food. The body has a way of compensating naturally for our lack of appetite-we usually don't feel like exerting much energy when we are sick. Our bodies are busy fighting whatever virus is attacking us and we're in standby mode. If you pay careful attention to the way your body feels and really begin to get in tune with its signals, you will learn to work with your body, instead of against it. Remember those " I can't believe I ate the WHOLLLE thing" commercials for Alka Seltzer? The poor guy rubbing his bulging belly because he went too far? You're eating to balance the amount of energy you are expending. If you "eat the whole thing" and you're not running the NYC marathon, chances are you are eating way too much and you'll feel sick. I haven't eaten the whole thing in years!

Michael, my brother-in-law, says that other than one period in high school when he was a bit heavy, he has been pleased with his weight for over 30 years. He warns that he knows he would not be able to maintain it if he did not exercise consistently 5-6 days a week. In addition, Michael adds that he is careful not to overeat. He generally eats out twice a week and brings his lunch to work every day. I admire him. He knows his body and he acts accordingly.

I've learned to recognize the need for balance on a daily basis. I don't obsess about it, but I am usually aware of what kind of day I'm having, exercise-wise and thus what kind of nutritional and caloric needs must be met. There is a really great smart phone app called My Fitness Pal, that helps you to compute how many calories you should be taking in on a given day, considering your weight, height, age, activity level, etc. It also can pull up the nutritional content of most of the foods that you eat, brand names and all. I tried it for a week straight and was absolutely appalled to see how many grams of sugar I was really eating. Twice as much as I was shooting for! There is always room for improvement... Anyhow, you can pull up the website too and investigate-I find it helpful and actually kind of fun.

Vegetable Barley soup that I sort of borrowed and changed from Mario Batali

Prep time 1:30

3 tbsp extra virgin olive oil

2 celery stalks thinly sliced

1 med white onion sliced thin

1 med leek, pale green and white parts only

1 tbsp tomato paste

½ c barley

2 quarts water

one 15 oz can small white beans, drained and rinsed

2 large carrots, cut ¼ inch thick

1 ½ c frozen peas

2 cups chopped kale

salt and pepper and fresh basil to taste

Heat oil in large stockpot. Add celery and leeks and cook until softened- 5 minutes. Add barley, bay leaves and tomato paste- cook 30 sec until barley is coated and shiny. Add 1 qt water and beans and bring to boil. Simmer on low for 30 min. Add carrots and 1 qt water. Cover and cook on low heat until carrots are tender, 30 min. Add peas and chopped kale and cook 5 minutes. Season with salt and pepper and top with basil leaves.

* Mario Batali uses faro, which I have a tough time finding, even in NYC, so I use barley instead. I also add kale at the end.

CHAPTER TEN

The Mindful Day

At the beginning of the book, I described to you what might happen on a given day when I am not eating mindfully, when my weaknesses come out, and I make a series of poor decisions. Now that you've had a little taste of my mindful eating philosophy, let's take a look at how I could have made a few tweaks given the same set of circumstances, and had a more nutritionally sound and successful day.

1. 7:05 am. My apartment. I'm starving and while I wait for the water in the shower to get warm, I forego the whoopee pie staring at me in the fridge and start my day with a half of a banana. It's sweet but it has some fiber and vitamins, including lots of potassium.

2. 7:25am. Time for breakfast. I go for the cereal, as usual, and because I only stock my cupboards with low-sugar, multigrain selections, I can only make a good decision. I am careful not to over pour from the box, as my eyes are often bigger than my stomach. I put about a ¾ cup size serving in my bowl. The cereal looks sad and meager, so I chop up about ¼ cup strawberries and throw in a few blue berries before adding what is probably 1/3 cup 1% organic milk. I never like seeing my cereal float. When I'm out of milk, I add ½ c fat free plain Greek yogurt to the cereal that ups my protein intake.

3. 8:55 am. Knowing I have a meeting first thing in the morning where they serve pastries and coffee, I make sure to get to my office early and fix myself a cup of hot rooibus tea and a snack. I have had the foresight to bring in some Fit For Life sprouted whole grains bread and spread a

tablespoon of all natural peanut butter on it and bring it with me up to the meeting. If I've got something satisfying nutritionally, I find I'm less likely to reach for the sugar.

4. 10:45 am. I am starving. I saunter into my colleague's office and discover that there is baklava and French bread with jam for the taking. Unlike in my earlier scenario of the unmindful day, I have remembered to bring some plain fat-free Greek yogurt and remind myself that I also have a bit of Kind peanut butter granola in my desk drawer. I take a tiny bite of the baklava, just a nibble, and go back to my office. I fill a cup with about 4 or 5 oz of yogurt and then sprinkle about two tablespoons of granola into it for some texture and sweetness. I like Kind because they make fairly healthy granolas lots of whole grains and without too much added sugar. Even so, I limit myself to just a couple of spoons, which is really all I need to give the yogurt some flavor.

5. 12:45 pm. Because I've been eating protein-rich, high-fiber snacks, I don't feel desperately hungry, but I know I have a 1:30 meeting, so I'd better get some lunch while I can. I go straight for the salad bar today; I don't even look at what is on the menu in the cafeteria. Time is of the essence and I want to make solid, smart easy choices. I take some romaine and mesculin greens, broccoli, carrots, tomatoes, a palm-sized amount of grilled chicken strips and a tablespoon of the quinoa salad. I sprinkle a small spoon of raisins and about a tablespoon of grated Parmesan cheese on top. I then take about a tablespoon of olive oil and a little less than that of balsamic vinegar and pour it on my salad. Done. I've got vitamins, fiber, protein, good fats (olive oil), and a modicum of "bad fats", cheese and a little bit of sugar in the raisins. I drink water with my salad and do not have bread or chips.

When I finish my lunch, which I have taken care to eat slowly, over a 20-minute period of time, I am reminded that Chris made those delicious lemon bars. I walk over to his desk and cut one into quarters and take one fourth of one of his sweet and delectable treats. I am very pleased with myself. I am certain that someone will later on be thankful for my surgical intervention on the lemon bar.

6. 2:45 pm. I have been asked to join some celebratory nurses in a round of Happy Birthday on one of the inpatient units. I would not change the part about how I sing the harmony, because that's just what I do. In my more mindful day, however, I realize I have had plenty of sweets already, and instead of taking even a small slice of the seven layer chocolate cake with butter cream frosting, I opt for just a forkful of a colleague's piece and I am on my way. Damn, that's good.

7. 4:30 pm. Feeling I need a little something to get me through the last half hour or so of the workday, I reach into my desk drawer and pull out some raw almonds and help myself to a small handful, maybe 10 almonds and a small rectangular piece of dark (72% cacao) chocolate, about one inch by one half inch. Low carb, high fiber, some fat, protein and just a tiny bit of sugar in the dark chocolate. That's how I like to snack.

8. 6:20 pm. I am on my way home from work and realize I haven't gone grocery shopping yet this week so I won't have much for dinner at home. I stop at Tony's take-out and decide a salad and some grilled chicken would be the best idea. I am slightly tempted by the breaded and fried cutlet, but know it will be no friend to my tummy, so I opt for the plain, grilled lemon chicken cutlet. It's about the size of two of my hands, so likely it will be enough for two servings and I can bring the rest for lunch

tomorrow. I don't rely on whatever wilted greens may or may not be lurking in my vegetable crisper at home, and also take an arugula, endive and tomato salad to go and ask for no dressing so I can mix my own at home.

After I'm home and have dined, I realize I'm quite full from a day of well-planned nutritional moves, so I don't even think about dessert. I do, however, always like to at least clean my mouth at the end of a meal with a little something sweet or fresh, so I wash off a few strawberries and enjoy them.

9. 8:00 pm. Ok, now I want a snack. It's the downside of having a quick metabolism and also not a large capacity for food in general. I want to be smart and not eat something heavy or sugary being that sleep is just a couple hours away. I take a half-cup of plain fat-free Greek yogurt and mix in just one *teaspoon* of Haagen Dazs chocolate peanut butter ice cream, just to

give it some flavor. It tastes like a rich dessert but it's mostly fat-free yogurt.

If you compare the judgment I used in the first chapter of the book, "The Unmindful Day", to the decisions I have made here given similar choices, you can see that with a bit of effort and common sense, it is not difficult to make sound picks that leave you feeling well-nourished and satisfied, instead of empty and disgusted. What is required is simply that you think twice before hand goes to mouth. You wouldn't put just anything in the gas tank of your car, would you? No. You fuel it with what keeps it working best and with what gives your car the greatest longevity. Why not do that for your body? Peace out (I don't know that I can pull that off, but I felt like saying it).

A Few Final Thoughts/Reminders:

1. Myfitnesspal.com - Love this app/website. You can record just about any food in your food diary and it will populate the nutritional value. You can also enter your own recipes for it to remember. The app keeps track of how much protein, carbs, sugars, protein, fat, calories you've had for the day as well as some key nutrients and how much is allowable for someone your size, weight, age, activity level. It also allows you to enter exercise done, which gives you more calories!

2. Kind Bars. A relatively low sugar alternative for a snack bar. Packed with protein and mostly all whole ingredients. Great quick energy snacks that won't send you into a sugar coma.

3. Smoothies made with low or non-fat Greek yogurt, natural peanut butter, skim milk, blueberries, a small piece of banana and a tiny dash of cocoa powder or raw cacao are a great alternative to a milk shake and much more satisfying.

4. I tend to eat most of my calories earlier in the day (before 4 or 5), so I'm content and not hungry later on and can just have a light meal for dinner. It's easier on my digestion too, to not have a lot to work on while I'm sleeping.

5. Each day is a brand new chance to eat sensibly. It doesn't matter if yesterday was a bust. Today can be the first day of lifetime of mindful eating for YOU.

6. Talk to your physician and or a dietician if you have health issues which need to be taken into account when considering a balanced diet that is right for you.

About the Author

Karen Wexler is a health advocate, writer and an actress who has appeared in theatre, film and television. Karen has written for hospital publications and was invited to present at the National Patient Safety Conference in 2013. She works as a patient representative in a NYC hospital and resides in Brooklyn, NY. "Having My Cake" marks the author's first book.

www.ingramcontent.com/pod-product-compliance
Lightning Source LLC
Chambersburg PA
CBHW060013050426
42448CB00012B/2738